DUTCH
FEAST

DUTCH FEAST

EMILY WIGHT

Arsenal Pulp Press

Vancouver

DUTCH FEAST
Copyright © 2017 by Emily Wight

ARSENAL PULP PRESS
Suite 202–211 East Georgia St.
Vancouver, BC V6A 1Z6
Canada
arsenalpulp.com

The publisher gratefully acknowledges the support of the Government of Canada, and the Government of British Columbia (through the Book Publishing Tax Credit Program), for its publishing activities.

Canada

The author and publisher assert that the information contained in this book is true and complete to the best of their knowledge. All recommendations are made without the guarantee on the part of the author and publisher. The author and publisher disclaim any liability in connection with the use of this information. For more information, contact the publisher.

Note for our UK readers: measurements for non-liquids are for volume, not weight.

Design by Oliver McPartlin
Interior and cover food photographs by Tracey Kusiewicz/Foodie Photography
Additional photography by Daria Yakovleva (p.193, 233, 239) and Leon Woods (p.237)

Edited by Susan Safyan

Printed and bound in Canada

Library and Archives Canada Cataloguing in Publication:
Wight, Emily, 1983-, author
        Dutch feast / Emily Wight.
Issued in print and electronic formats.
ISBN 978-1-55152-687-4 (hardcover).–ISBN 978-1-55152-688-1 (PDF)
        1. Cooking, Dutch. 2. Cookbooks. I. Title.
TX723.5.N4W53 2017   641.59492   C2017-904035-9
                                               C2017-904036-7

To Hunter and Hudson: Never turn down an offer of food or the opportunity to travel. You'll never regret wandering off in search of snacks and adventure, though you may regret inviting me to go with you.

CONTENTS

INTRODUCTION

If you don't know much about Dutch cuisine, it might be easy to assume that there is not much to it. If you've only been to Amsterdam, for example, you might guess that the primary dishes of the Netherlands are French fries and mayonnaise or bitterballen and mustard. Perhaps if you grew up in a Dutch household with diasporic parents, your association with Dutch food may be the boiled mushes and stewed meats or sausages that make up an infinite variety of stamppots, potato-based dishes of mashed veggies meant to serve as the basis for an infinite variety of stewed, fried, or tube meats. You might even be forgiven for thinking that it is a lot like British food—bland, boiled, occasionally deep-fried, and that's about it.

I promise you, even when it is boiled and/or deep-fried, that is not all there is to it. (Which is not to minimize the Dutch affinity for boiling and mashing things; boiled mushes are a fundamental part of Dutch cuisine, but they are nourishing and delicious and often oozing with butter and/or gravy—see "Stamppots," page 173.)

The Netherlands is comprised of twelve provinces and borders Germany and Belgium (the United Kingdom is across the water, and France not too far away). At various points in history, the British and the French have been—or have viewed the Dutch as—antagonists. The northern Dutch, in the area known as Friesland, claim—and history supports this—that English and Friese are related dialects; Friese

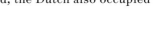

and Old English share similar-sounding words that look quite different from other Germanic dialects.

Additionally, there are three special municipalities: Bonaire, Sint Eustatius, and Saba, which are part of the Netherlands proper and participate in Dutch and European elections despite being located in the Caribbean—they are regarded in much the same way as any municipality on the mainland, though they do not comprise their own distinct province. In addition, the Kingdom of the Netherlands also includes the Caribbean islands of Aruba, Curaçao, and Sint Maarten, which are independently governed but still economically tied to the Netherlands proper. Prior to the end of their colonial period, the Dutch also occupied

Indonesia, Suriname, Brazil, Sri Lanka, India, and parts of Africa, though they were not always successful in maintaining their holdings against the British, Portuguese, and Spanish. Early migrants to North America established New Netherland in what are now the mid-Atlantic States of New York, New Jersey, Delaware, and Connecticut; their presence in the area established what would later become essential elements of American culture and cuisine, including coleslaw, pancakes, doughnuts, and apple pie.

The Dutch culinary tradition is very diverse, and whatever you might think of Dutch food today, Dutch people have always enjoyed good quality local ingredients, often prepared simply. They benefit from a temperate, coastal climate, a diverse variety of agricultural products, and a commercial greenhouse industry that produces fruits and vegetables year-round. Meat, dairy products, and fish are abundant. There is so much bread—and it is such good bread.

Sweets and pastries are important to Dutch cuisine and are not necessarily dessert; often, a piece of vlaai (tart) is served with coffee in the middle of the day. Pies and tarts are not too sweet and quite sturdy—often served with a generous dollop (okay, a heap) of whipped cream. Whipped cream appears as a dessert topping more frequently than ice cream, and it is a very good quality, high-fat cream that melts slowly into the crevices of hot desserts or is spooned off warm chocolademelk like pudding. Cookies are often crisp and firm, meant to stand up to a hot cup of coffee. In the evening, a Dutch family might enjoy

vla, a fresh, dairy-based pudding, poured from a carton kept in the refrigerator.

Dutch cooking is commonly defined by thriftiness and practicality, and while often hearty and rich with butter and cheese, it is nourishing and healthful. It relies on inexpensive ingredients that are widely available—apples, potatoes, Belgian and curly endive, onions, and kale feature prominently—with interesting combinations of spices and flavorings to add character and taste. It is a cuisine influenced by its colonial history, with bold flavors coming from places like Indonesia and Suriname, and by its proximity to its neighbors, especially Belgium. Flavor preferences often lean sweet and salty, and common spices include nutmeg, anise, and coriander. Historically, a delicate hand with flavors such as rose water, vanilla, and saffron have lent an air of sophistication to otherwise simple dishes.

I am a little defensive about Dutch food, partly because, for whatever reason, it has not been given its due internationally. We talk about the food of the Netherlands' neighbors a fair bit—Belgian food is practically French, after all (don't tell them I said that), and German food has been increasingly celebrated in recent years—everyone knows about schnitzel, there are a million food blogger recipes for spaetzli (literally more than a million if you type "spaetzle" into Google right now)—and in any grocery store anywhere, you can find Bratwurst or Weisswurst or Liverwurst. Even British food—which we used to talk about as mostly grey boiled slop—has seen a renaissance. But you can't really malign a whole country's cuisine without giving it a fair shake, and there is more to Dutch cuisine than meets the eye. A nation of tall, healthy, happy people does not spring from a gastronomic wasteland.

One factor, I think, is tourism.

"Many visitors come to Amsterdam with a list of things to do while here: get high, motorboat a hooker, that sort of thing," said chef and writer Anthony Bourdain during a 2012 episode of his Travel Channel show *The Layover*. I think that's probably got a lot to do with the perception of the nation's food—really, if you're visiting a country to get your kicks in a way you're not allowed to back home, is a culinary pilgrimage really a part of that? And, it's true, the Netherlands is a socially liberal place where you can get into all sorts of trouble if that's what you're hoping to do. But the trains run well, and the cities are well connected, and leaving downtown Amsterdam to eat beyond tourist fare is something that I think people would find real value in.

When visitors to the Netherlands talk about Dutch food, they mention the idiosyncratic elements, the novelties—things like the aggressively salty licorice or the vending-machine croquettes. But there's so much more than that, even in downtown Amsterdam. The Indonesian food is incredible. You can find a rare glimpse of Surinamese food, a cuisine—also, for reasons I don't understand—not well known beyond Suriname itself and the Kingdom of the Netherlands. And the breads and cookies and cakes are arguably some of the most interesting and delicious in Western Europe. In his book *An Embarrassment of Riches*, scholar and historian Simon Schama describes the Dutch appetite in the Golden Age (roughly spanning the seventeenth century) as interpreted through paintings and historical accounts: "The Dutch, it was thought by most other European contemporaries, did not pick at their victuals. In caricatures they were almost always depicted as guzzlers and sozzlers, as imposingly broad as they were dauntingly tall." You do not get to guzzling and sozzling if your food is boring. You just don't.

Another factor, I think, is the Dutch diaspora.

Aside from the occasional pannekoeken (pancake) house, you just don't see a lot of Dutch cuisine in North America. Part of that is because the early influence of Dutch people on North American cuisine is largely invisible—what Dutch people brought to America became American in a way that food from other cultures did not necessarily, and so in many ways their contribution to the canon of western cuisine has been erased. Dutch immigrants arrived in waves, and the later waves, especially those who arrived in Canada and the United States after World War II, were keen to integrate and become Canadian or American. And where people did maintain their connections to the homeland, they did so quietly, in clusters—in their churches, in Christian school communities, in neighborhoods where other Dutch families settled. There are stores for Dutch groceries, but there are very few of them. Dutch parents came to North America and then didn't get their children Dutch passports. Dutch cuisine was relegated to a few key meals—boerenkool (mashed potatoes with kale) and sausage or the annual olliebollen (sweet, deep-fried dumplings) at New

Year's, or a few croquettes at the annual church Christmas Bazaar.

Dutch immigrants began emigrating to North America in the seventeenth century, first arriving on the east coast of the United States in 1614. Early migrants were largely concentrated around New Netherland. Following a rift in the church over theological liberalism in the nineteenth century, many members of the Dutch Reform Church left the Netherlands for Canada and the United States, settling in Ontario, Alberta, and British Columbia (in Canada), and in the American Midwest, with large concentrations of people with Dutch ancestry in Iowa, Michigan, Illinois, and Wisconsin.

Canadians in particular were regarded highly by the Dutch; it was the Canadians who liberated the Netherlands from the Germans in 1945. After the war, waves of Dutch migrants began arriving in Canada, partly in pursuit of better opportunities, with Dutch immigration peaking in the early 1950s. My partner Nick's grandparents (known as Pake and Beppe) came to Canada in 1952. (Nick's family hails from the northern Dutch province of Friesland. Hunter—who I will talk about a fair bit, especially in relation to pancakes and chocolate—is our son; he is five and usually covered in sugar.)

The last factor, I think, is the Dutch themselves.

A common Dutch expression is "doe normaal," which means "be normal." It is impolite—vulgar, even—to brag or to make oneself the center of attention; it is perhaps this element of the collective Dutch personality that emphasizes fitting in, even abroad, even in completely new territory. This urge to not call too much attention to oneself may be why we don't go to Dutch pubs for borrels (kind of like Dutch tapas) in Vancouver, or grab stamppot on the way home from work in Seattle. There are over 16 million people of Dutch heritage outside the Netherlands, and the fact that we don't know more about Dutch cuisine is probably most attributable to Dutch humility and reluctance to boast about themselves.

On occasion, my enthusiasm for Dutch cuisine has come up in conversation with people from Dutch backgrounds, and overwhelmingly they have responded incredulously. "How many recipes for boiled mush can you put into a book?" From children of Dutch parents to drunk Dutchmen at wedding receptions to Dutch grad students in the labs and lunch queues at the university where I work, everyone asks the same question: "What is Dutch food, anyway?" And I can point to specific dishes, and we can talk about their favorite meals or treats, but ultimately, the question remains: what is Dutch cuisine? Fortunately, I have no problem boasting and am occasionally distressingly vulgar, and so I don't mind telling you.

Dutch cuisine is wholesome, economical, and stubbornly delicious. The thing that always baffles me is that most Dutch cuisine is on a par with what we would consider modern western food—the elegant breads, the global influences, the good-quality ingredients, and the liberal use of spices; it's all the kind of thing you'd see in *Bon Appetit*, but Dutch people just don't talk about it or think to hold it up in comparison to what is new and trendy right now. Dutch cuisine is inspired by local, seasonal ingredients, international flavors, and a profound love for sugar; dairy products and breads feature prominently, and cheese is a source of national pride. In short, Dutch cuisine is approachable, comforting, and accessible for the home cook—practicality is a pillar of the national character, and food is impractical if it is not both nourishing and delicious. And it is delicious, and it is nourishing, and I would fly you there with me so I could show you all my favorite dishes firsthand, but for now, this book will have to do.

If you're looking for highlights with which to begin your explorations in Dutch cooking, I recommend:

- Suikerbrood (sugar bread), page 39
- Boeterkoek (butter cake), specifically Beppe's, page 56
- Bitterballen (small croquettes), page 76
- Pom (a casserole made with potatoes and chicken), page 117
- Spicy Prawns with Green Beans, page 160
- Mosterdsoep (mustard soup), page 184
- Rijstebrij (rice pudding), page 226

The recipes in this book are a mix of traditional Dutch recipes, reimagined or modernized Dutch recipes, and adaptations of Dutch recipes designed to use items in the pantry list that follows. Rather than stick to tradition in the case of adapted recipes, I have worked to ensure that if there is an ingredient in a recipe where it is of critical importance, then it has been worked into other recipes so that you are not stuck with something you made a special trip to the store for and then will never use again. For most of us, cupboard space is at a premium, so we have no room for one-offs; I would rather that these recipes fit easily into your routine than have them adhere to a tradition that even Dutch people themselves might not feel beholden to. Practicality first, always.

And always, *always* eet smajkelik!

A Timeline of Dutch Cuisine

1300–1600: There isn't a lot of information about the cuisine of the European lowlands prior to the twelfth century, but we do know that there was cheese. Dairy products have long been a staple of the cuisine of the region, and by the seventeenth century, the Netherlanders began to be known for their cheese and butter. Dutch fisherman discovered that salting fish preserved them, opening up the herring export industry and strengthening the Dutch fishing economy. Beer production was also expanded and industrialized. The early stages of colonial expansion began, and trade routes and outposts were established in the East.

1600–1800: With an abundance and variety of fresh ingredients and a stack of new cookbooks available to literate households, Dutch cuisine became increasingly formalized as a canon of recipes took shape. Spices, sugar, dried fruits, rice, and other international products were available to wealthier consumers. Eating became a pleasurable social affair for the upper classes. Referred to as the Golden Age, this was a period of abundance in the Netherlands, with protein, including meats, fish, and cheese, available to even the working classes. The art of the time showcased elaborate, expensive ingredients that would have been hard to come by for anyone but the very rich, including oranges, lemons, grapes, and olives.

The Dutch East India Company was established and the occupation of Indonesia began. The Dutch come to be leaders in the slave trade in Europe, exploiting the potential of the sugar industry in parts of South America and the Caribbean. Dutch processing is invented, changing cocoa and expanding its utility.

1800–1950: For poorer families, this was a challenging period in Dutch cuisine, and one during which potatoes become a staple of the national diet. The Dutch expanded their presence in Indonesia until World War II, when they lost the territory to Japan. Following the war and Indonesian independence, a wave of Indonesian migrants began to establish homes in the Netherlands, opening restaurants and influencing the taste of Dutch home cooking.

1950–2000s: Dutch cuisine shifts to a more modest style with an emphasis on thriftiness and nutrition. Traditional recipes are modernized and simplified. As more women work outside the home, home cooking begins to change as well. Potatoes remain integral to Dutch cuisine, with stamppots regularly served at the Dutch table. Modern Dutch cuisine favors balance and moderation, with room for a few treats throughout the day.

STOCKING YOUR DUTCH KITCHEN

The Dutch pantry is diverse, but you will use the ingredients over and over. The Dutch kitchen is well-stocked with spices, sauces, extracts, and condiments to add bold flavor to simple, often seasonal ingredients. Buy good spices in small amounts in order to keep costs down and ensure that spices are always fresh. I buy my spices from a local bulk foods store or from an Indian grocery nearby.

SPICES, DRIED

Allspice
Allspice is not, in fact, all spices, but it is actually a dried berry that looks a bit like a large peppercorn. Allspice, sometimes known as pimienta, smells like a combination of nutmeg, cloves, and cinnamon, and is commonly used in Dutch baking. It is also used widely in Caribbean cuisines.

Cinnamon
If you are concerned about using the very best cinnamon, look for Ceylon cinnamon in gourmet or specialty stores. If you are concerned about price, regular cinnamon, which is not really cinnamon but cassia bark, will do just fine. Cinnamon is one of the things I can't be a fundamentalist about, because most people buy supermarket cinnamon and don't know any different. This is not the hill that I will die on, but if cinnamon authenticity is important to you, by all means splurge. Be sure to buy both ground cinnamon and cinnamon sticks. I store my cinnamon sticks in the freezer to keep them fresh.

Cloves
Cloves can be offensive in large amounts, but a hint of clove is lovely and makes things taste like Christmas. Buy a small container of ground cloves, and a small bag of whole cloves as well.

Coriander
For the purposes of this book, and because I hail from North America, when we're talking about coriander here, we're talking about the seeds. When calling for the leaves, I call for cilantro. When calling for coriander, what you want is that sort of earthy, floral flavor that the seeds give. Coriander pairs very well with citrus and fresh herbs.

Cumin
Cumin tastes good and is one of those spices that exists in the background of many cuisines, a fundamental component of a number of spice blends but also a standalone ingredient. Part of the same family of plants that parsley comes from, cumin has a warm, peppery, almost onion-y

flavor, making it a popular ingredient in cuisines throughout the world.

Curry powder, yellow

Curry powder is essential—it's a "do-it-all" spice that is widely frowned-upon by food snobs who clearly don't know any better, but a reliable go-to in the kitchen of moms everywhere. I prefer Madras curry powder, which is a mix of cumin, coriander, turmeric, cinnamon, fenugreek, cardamom, chili powder, and curry leaves. I buy it at a local Indian supermarket chain. Use what you prefer—I like mine a little hotter, but if all you have access to is the regular supermarket stuff, it will do just fine for the recipes that follow. I call it "yellow curry powder" descriptively, so that you know you are not looking for garam masala, which has a fundamentally different taste and color.

Fennel seeds

Fennel seeds are sweet and reminiscent of licorice, more herbaceous than anise, another licorice-like flavor, and a valuable addition to savory and sweet dishes alike. Toast until golden in a dry pan or skillet on medium-high heat before using in recipes.

Ginger

Ground ginger has a sweeter, earthier taste than fresh ginger and is a necessary element of many

Stroopwaffles

Dutch baked goods. While fresh ginger is delightful and important to many dishes, it is not a substitute for powdered dried ginger.

Nutmeg

Nutmeg is a workhorse in Dutch cuisine; it's absolutely essential. And while the recipes here call for ground nutmeg, I highly recommend buying nutmeg whole and grating it finely with a rasp or microplane, as the flavor stays fresh for quite a lot longer. Freshly ground nutmeg is nutty and fragrant, with a sort of woodsy, spicy note that works well in baked goods or dairy-based dishes.

Paprika

Paprika is a popular flavor in Europe, especially the Netherlands; bell peppers (capsicum) are called "paprika," and everything from Doritos to fancy cheese comes in paprika flavor. While many Dutch recipes call for paprika generally, and most likely refer to the sweet Hungarian kind, I think smoked Spanish paprika works very well in most Dutch dishes, adding a savory note and depth of flavor, especially to those that are pork- or sausage-based. Unless otherwise specified, choose smoked Spanish paprika for your pantry.

Pepper, black

Like nutmeg, pepper is best fresh-ground. Buy whole peppercorns and a grinder that is comfortable to use, and you will never need pre-ground pepper again.

Saffron

Good saffron has a smell a little like sweet pepper, and reminds me a bit of anise, not because of its fragrance but because of the way both are sweet and bitter at the same time. Good saffron is expensive, but you can get a lot of flavor out of not very much of the spice. To get the most mileage out of it, grind a pinch with a mortar and pestle (if you don't have that, use your thumb and grind into the palm of your other hand) along with a pinch of sugar, then steep in ½ cup (250mL) hot water. The result is a saffron extract. Where I call for "a pinch of saffron," feel free to use about a tablespoon of the extract. This mixture will allow you to use saffron in multiple recipes. Keep in mind that saffron blooms—releases its color and flavor—in water but does not bloom as successfully in fat. Look for saffron in stores that sell Italian or Persian groceries.

Saffron

Salt, kosher

For consistency of flavor, wherever salt is called for, I mean kosher salt, a non-iodized, coarse-grained salt. I use Windsor coarse kosher salt, a Canadian brand that is similar to Morton's, at about 14 g (0.5 oz) per tablespoon.

I also think salt preferences are very personal, so wherever I have called for X-amount of salt, please don't feel constrained by that; I think we all salt to taste, so please do not blow up my DMs if you think two teaspoons of salt is nowhere near enough to make something delicious and you believe I have failed you. (I am seventy percent talking to just Nick here, who has a lot of opinions that I am forced to ignore.) Always salt to taste.

Star anise

Star anise is pretty and has a sweet, woodsy, licorice-like flavor. It is native to Vietnam and other parts of Southeast Asia. Buy it whole or in pieces for optimal flavor; ground star anise loses its flavor quickly.

Turmeric

Turmeric is magic—research has begun to show that compounds found in turmeric may be beneficial in shrinking tumors, reducing inflammation, and fighting the effects of some autoimmune diseases. In food, it is useful in turning things yellow; it has a very mild, sort of peppery taste that is subtle in small amounts.

SPICES, FRESH

Chilies

While most Dutch cuisine is not very spicy, chilies do liven up the occasional dish, especially at a rijsttafel (pronounced "rice-taffel"). I find, for guests who are not inclined toward chilies, that jalapeños and serranos are an easy, not *too* spicy place to start. A couple of recipes in this book will call for very spicy Thai bird chilies, but if you are not down with the hotness, a milder chili will do. If you want some of the taste but less of the heat, halve chilies and remove the membrane (the white pithy bit) and seeds. Use gloves, and avoid touching your eyes.

Ginger

Fresh ginger is the base—with garlic and onions—of most delicious curries. Look for ginger that is plump and thin-skinned; it should not appear shriveled or woody. Fresh ginger minces easily and smells fresh; once it begins to dry out, it can be fibrous and harder to work with.

Lemongrass

Fresh lemongrass has become quite popular in recent years and is now available in most supermarkets, often near the herbs. If you can't find lemongrass in your usual supermarket, try a local Asian market; if you can't find it there, you can often find preserved lemongrass, trimmed stalks in jars, in the International aisle. Lemongrass gives an herbal, citrus taste and a fresh, zingy fragrance.

If you track down a good deal, you can store trimmed stalks in the freezer for up to six months.

Lime leaves

The leaves of the makrut lime have been increasingly available in grocery stores over the past couple of years; look for them near the "specialty" produce, like galangal, fresh turmeric, peeled garlic, or jackfruit. The leaves can also be found in Asian supermarkets. Often they are packaged in-store to keep them fresh longer. If you can't find fresh lime leaves, you may be able to find them frozen. If you do end up with more fresh leaves than you can use, freeze for up to six months.

Lime Leaves

FLAVORINGS
Almond extract

Almond extract features prominently in many North American interpretations of traditional Dutch recipes, as it mimics the taste of hard-to-find almond paste in some baked goods. Pure almond extract is generally pretty inexpensive—you don't need to splurge on this.

Anise extract

This extract is very strong, and I use it in place of anise seeds in baking and ice cream. As with rose water, a little goes a long way.

Brandy

Dutch brandy doesn't contain grapes, and is usually made from grain or sugar (molasses) liquor. It can be hard to find in North America, so regular brandy will work just fine.

Gin

For the purposes of this book, I have referred to gin where a Dutch cook might use genever, because genever can be hard to source in some places. I have also used gin instead of juniper as a seasoning in some cases, as juniper can also be hard to find.

Rose water

Before the arrival of vanilla, Dutch bakers and cooks used rose water to flavor everything from cakes and cookies to egg dishes. A little rose water goes a long way, so a bottle should last you a good long time; I get my rose water for under $3 per bottle at a local Persian foods shop. Rose water works very well with berries, and I love it with rhubarb (see Rosy Rhubarb Preserve, page 243).

Rum

Rum is used as a flavoring in a number of desserts, from vla to klappertaart (coconut cake), the latter a dessert inspired by the Dutch that originated in Indonesia. You can buy rum extract, but I like to keep a bottle of inexpensive rum in the freezer for cooking. And other stuff.

Vanilla extract

Vanilla is a popular flavoring for puddings, yogurts, and desserts in Dutch cuisine; often, recipes will call for a whole vanilla bean. This can get expensive, as vanilla prices have surged due to climate change in recent years, so I recommend buying the best real vanilla you can afford. (I like vanilla bean paste, which I buy in tubs for a volume discount.) One vanilla bean equals one teaspoon vanilla extract. Artificial vanilla is a garbage product that I cannot recommend.

CONDIMENTS, SAUCES, AND SYRUPS

Note: See also recipes in Condiments & Preserves, pp. 235-251.

Fish sauce

This one is controversial. Or, at the very least, an inauthentic substitution in most cases. In many Dutch-Indonesian dishes, cooks use trassi, a pungent fermented shrimp paste the strong taste of which largely disappears during cooking (leaving only a satisfying umami flavor behind). Sold in the Netherlands in blocks or powder, it can be hard to come by in North America. One substitution for trassi is anchovy paste, but I find that the fish sauce I have on hand for other things works just fine (and is available in most supermarkets).

Ketjap manis

Ketjap manis (also spelled kecap manis) is a hugely important ingredient in Indonesian and Indo-Dutch cuisine. It's a thick, sweet soy sauce that's fundamental to a great many dishes, including those in this book. Some supermarkets still don't stock it, but you can find it in Asian markets or online; it's worth seeking out, and fairly inexpensive. While you can make it yourself (and if you need to make it gluten-free, try the recipe on page 246), I think you'll find it worth seeking out. There's a Dutch brand—Conimex—but I don't like it and it's too expensive; I prefer ABC brand, which will cost you about $5 USD for a 620-mL (21-oz) bottle.

Maggi

A sweet, salty, soy-based product used throughout the world, Maggi is liquid umami, and we have a rule around here that Nick is not allowed to just pour it into everything without tasting the dish first. Widely used in Asia, it's actually a Swiss product and much beloved in places like the Netherlands and Germany. Nick insists that every soup is better with a few generous drops.

Mustard

Typical Dutch mustard is somewhere between French Dijon and American yellow in taste and color. It can be hard to find in North America, but a grainy Dijon mustard works just fine. If you're ordering online, Zaanse Molen Dutch Mustard is a good option. Use it in salad dressings, sauces, soups, and as a regular old condiment.

Sambal oelek

Sambal oelek is a mother sauce in our home; it goes into everything. It's made of hot red chili peppers and salt and sometimes vinegar; put it in stews and soups for warmth and spice, or dollop it on eggs or avocado toast to cure your hangover. My favorite application is sambal green beans, where sautéed green beans are simply tossed in sambal oelek in the pan; we eat these with white rice and roast chicken.

Sambal oelek

Soy sauce

I feel like this is probably pretty self-explanatory. However, in addition to regular soy sauce, I like to keep a bottle of gluten-free soy sauce on hand for dinner guests who have Celiac disease or are gluten intolerant.

Stroop

Stroop is a thick, dark syrup that is lot like molasses, and for the purposes of this book, wherever one might traditionally use stroop, I have substituted fancy molasses, the kind most often used for baking. For pancakes, a lighter version of stroop exists; this is similar to cane sugar syrup, such as Rogers Golden Syrup or Lyle's, which you can find in the baking section of the supermarket.

DRIED FRUIT AND NUTS

Raisins, prunes, dried apricots, and dried figs have long been popular in the Netherlands; during the nineteenth century, some Dutch physicians thought that many dried fruits, like prunes, were healthier than their fresh counterparts. This is partly because it was thought that dried fruits were more digestible and less likely to cause bloating and discomfort. I am not sure which dried fruits those doctors were eating, but it's an interesting theory. "Exotic" dried-fruit treats like dates or candied ginger and fruit peel are commonly used in baking and to top yogurt or porridge.

Nuts, including hazelnuts, pistachios, almonds, walnuts, and peanuts, are commonly used in Dutch cuisine.

EGGS AND DAIRY

Eggs

When we talk about eggs in any of the recipes that follow, I mean large eggs. Large eggs contain about three and a half tablespoons of liquid; substituting another size egg may throw off the balance of a recipe, especially where moisture content is key. For consistency's sake, purchase large eggs.

Butter

I am a fan of unsalted butter for a number of reasons, but for consistency's sake when the recipes here refer to butter, it means *salted* butter. If you prefer and generally keep unsalted butter for cooking and baking, consider increasing the salt in a recipe by a quarter teaspoon.

Buttermilk

Buttermilk is a drink in the Netherlands, but it is also used in cooking. My preference is for full-fat buttermilk—at least three percent fat.

Cheese

There are many wonderful Dutch cheeses, and I wish we could talk about them all in detail, but there is a limited variety available in the North American market. *Dutch Feast* emphasizes cheeses you are most likely to find in grocery stores, mainly Edam and Gouda (young, smoked, and aged). For recipes that call for cheese to be fried, I have suggested medium Cheddar, but you can use any young, supermarket brick Gouda in place of Cheddar if you are a purist. I prefer mild, medium, or brick Gouda for recipes where meltiness or sliceability are important. (See p. 25.)

Milk and cream

The recipes call for whole milk and occasionally heavy cream. While milk-fat percentage doesn't seriously affect baking, I think a higher fat milk is preferable in puddings, soups, and beverages; look for milk that is at least three percent milk fat.

Depending where you live, heavy cream can be sold as whipping cream; look for a cream with at least thirty-five and up to forty percent milk fat.

Yogurt and sour cream

If you're sensing a theme here, it's that I think low-fat dairy is kind of pointless. I also think that low-fat yogurt and sour cream are gross. They are often starchy, because they don't thicken on their own and are packed with cornstarch or other stabilizers. Choose natural yogurts containing only milk ingredients and bacterial cultures, and look for a fat content between three and six percent. Sour cream should be around fourteen percent milk fat.

Recommended Equipment

Candy/deep-fry thermometer

If you are making candy, jam, or appelstroop, or deep-frying anything, an inexpensive glass candy thermometer that clips onto the side of a pot will save you all kinds of trouble. Aim to spend about eight dollars on one, and it will last you for decades. I stole mine from my mom ten years ago, and I have no idea how old it is. Hi, Mom! Sorry for everything.

Cast iron skillet, 12-in (30-cm)

Again, this doesn't have to be expensive. Lodge brand cast iron is a good value, and very sturdy; also check out outdoor supply stores, where cookware marketed for camp cooking can be cheaper than in kitchen supply or department stores.

Dutch oven

Look for a Dutch oven at least 12 inches (30 cm) in diameter. This will take you from stovetop to oven seamlessly, and doesn't have to be expensive—high-end brands are lovely, but you can buy a perfectly acceptable enameled cast iron pot for under fifty dollars. Shop around—some celebrity chef-branded products are decently priced and fair quality.

Food mill

If you enjoy mashed potatoes, velvety smooth soups, or making applesauce, a food mill will be invaluable for you. I bought a crappy one to see if I'd ever use it, and I used it so much it fell apart (and the handle melted). You should be able to find a good metal one for under fifty dollars; it will make a lot of your cooking quicker and better-textured. Trust me on this one.

Kitchen scale (optional)

A scale can be helpful in weighing produce, as fruits and veggies can be highly variable in size. Where I have called for one stalk of celery or one carrot, the weight doesn't matter, and a range of approximate volumes will suit the recipe. Where I have called for an ingredient by weight, it is because it matters to the outcome of the recipe; it's possible to weigh produce as you are buying it, using the scales in the supermarket. You can purchase an analog kitchen scale for under twenty dollars; if you're looking for more accurate measurements or intend to use a scale for measuring ingredients for baking, there are good digital scales available for around $25 USD.

Cheese

"The true destiny of the North Holland farmer's wife is cheesing, cheesing, always cheesing."
—Hildebrand (pseudonym of Nicolaas Beets, pastor and writer, 1841)

"I know you just went to the store, but we're out of cheese again—don't be mad."
—Nick VanderWoud, 2015

At a showcase of local businesses in a village that we visited in Friesland, I met the proprietor of Het Spijshuys, a Friese-Swiss restaurant in town, and he convinced me to buy his cheese. Not that it would have taken much convincing—the cheese was locally made and studded throughout with the restaurant's house-cured sausage. The sausage, also available for sale, was studded with the cheese. It was a beautiful, magical thing, and Nick and I ate it all one night, meaning to save some for another evening. Marry someone who'll indulge you in the occasional cheese binge and you'll have something you can enjoy together your whole lives. It's a lot more fun than golf or deep conversation.

The Netherlands and Belgium comprise what's known in Europe as the lowlands, a part of the continent that typically endured a lot of flooding. The Netherlands has historically been in a rather precarious position, with much of the country close to or, for about thirteen percent of the land, below sea level. Once the Dutch established their complicated system of dikes and pumps to control flooding and reduce the erosion of habitable land, they found that the marshy grasslands that resulted were great for grazing cattle. Not that cheese-making is recent—the region has produced cheese as far back as 400 AD.

Cheese is a source of national pride and has been a source of moral superiority—it's wholesome, domestic, and universally beloved. Even the Dutch Calvinist clergy of the seventeenth century, a decidedly un-fun group who saw the devil in anything enjoyable, thought cheese virtuous and humble. Dairy production was, and still is, a highlight of the Dutch economy, and milk products were abundant. Even the working classes had access to fresh milk, butter, and cheese, and in times of precarity, when clean drinking water was less available, people drank milk to stay hydrated (beer too, but that's a topic for another page—page 136, specifically).

There are a variety of Dutch cheeses, often named for their town of origin (e.g., Gouda or Edam). Some are flavored with spices, such as cloves or cumin, or with

vegetables, like kale, tomato, or onion. There are old cheeses and young cheeses and hard cheeses and even goat cheeses—there was a lavender goat's cheese in the Markthal (Market Hall) in Rotterdam that I kept sneaking samples of, and we would have bought some to take home with us if I hadn't already spent forty Euros on cheese and done the math on what that meant in Canadian dollars. A lot, let's just say. A lot.

The Netherlands produces more than 800,000 tons of cheese per year, and while they do export a good portion of that, they manage to eat quite a bit themselves, about forty-four pounds (twenty kilograms) per person, per year. Maybe that's why they're so tall? The average height for an adult man in the Netherlands is six feet (183 cm), and what's interesting is that you don't have to be genetically Dutch to achieve such height—even those from other genetic backgrounds who grow up in the Netherlands tend to be taller, even where average heights in their ancestral country skew lower. It's the cheese. I'm sure of it.

Most days, the average breakfast in the Netherlands would be a bit of cheese or butter on bread, a glass of buttermilk, and a cup of coffee. Lunch is much the same. After work, one might peruse the borrels on display at the supermarket and choose a plastic container of cheese cubes for a snack in the evening with a bit of gin, and then, before bed, a snack of cheese on roggebrood, a pumpernickel-like rye bread, with a slice of cheese and a glass of milk or tea might hit the spot. If there's a best way to live, I suspect the Dutch have it all figured out.

BREAKFAST

HANGOP WITH ROASTED
RHUBARB
32

RICE PANCAKES
33

CURRANT BREAD
35

BREAKFAST BREAD
36

SUGAR BREAD
39

BUTTERMILK RYE WAFFLES
40

APPLESAUCE RAISIN CAKE
42

SAFFRON MILK
44

STAR ANISE MILK
44

SWEET GERTIES
45

APPLE-RAISIN COMPOTE
46

OATMEAL WITH
DRIED FRUIT & ALMONDS
47

EGGS IN DUTCH LETTUCE
49

BREAKFAST

I am not a particularly motivated breakfast eater; I don't like to get up earlier than I need to, and I am not particularly personable before nine o'clock in the morning, so "What's for breakfast?" is the kind of question that makes me lash out irrationally (at least before I've had a pint of coffee). Nick is the same. We are monsters, but at least we worked out early on that nothing we say before breakfast is consequential.

Maybe my problem is that I'm not a particularly motivated breakfast-maker. Who is, though? Is it you? I would love to know how you do it, so long as it doesn't involve me having to eat a cold Mason jar full of sad oatmeal in almond milk before I have to field one million questions on the way to kindergarten drop-off and then at the office.

The Dutch are a practical people, and I think we can all agree that any kind of urgency in the morning is impractical. One must gird oneself against the demands of the day. Protecting your leisure time, even if it is just a few minutes first thing in the morning, is very important for your overall well-being, whether you are Dutch or not, and no one ever savored a moment cramming a granola bar into her mouth on the way to the car.

In general, the Netherlands aims to be progressive in terms of gender equality—in 1977, the Dutch government established an Emancipation Council to implement policies informed by feminist activists and female community leaders. However, despite efforts to bring gender equality to the working class, women still work part-time in far greater numbers in the Netherlands than in other western nations. And in my home, as modern and equality-minded as my own partner is, I do most of the work of preparing our family for the day, whether I want to or not, whether I am good at it or not. (My style of mothering is probably best described as always late and highly frazzled.) I can understand why a nation of women would be like, "Eh, bread's fine. Give the kids some hagelslaag and let's get moving."

In the Netherlands, the morning meal is mostly bread-based—either a couple of slices of spiced ontbijtkoek (breakfast cake) with a thick layer of butter, or a slice of bread, toasted or not, white or spelt, or studded with currants, and topped with a smear of butter, a thin slice of cheese, a boiled egg, some ham, maybe Nutella, maybe butter and jam. And, whenever Hunter is present, with peanut butter and hagelslaag (chocolate sprinkles). A bit of bread and coffee or tea and maybe a cloudy glass of apple juice is a pretty ideal way to start the day.

The Dutch will save a heartier breakfast for the weekend or a special occasion. On the weekend, a few eggs prepared simply, a bit of porridge with dried fruit, or a waffle and some cheese or stroop is perfectly lovely, and the kind of thing you could use to lure friends to your kitchen table with the promise of strong coffee.

When we journeyed up to Friesland to visit Nick's family, I watched as Nick's father's cousin bought no fewer than seven loaves of bread, ostensibly for the weekend, maybe just for our visit, but I don't think so. There was sugar bread with sticky, jammy bits of sugar melted into a gently spiced dough. There were crisp, crunchy rusks, like thicker melba toasts with a more appealing crumb—sturdy enough to support a runny egg or a bit of jam and hangop, but not so hard they'd hurt your teeth to chomp into. There were long loaves and short loaves and buns. And when we came down for breakfast—a little late, still jet-lagged—there were loaves of bread laid out for us, and every spread imaginable; spicy speculaas spread, peanut butter, Nutella, French jams, Dutch butter, and delicate rounds of ham and a huge hunk of cheese from which to drag as many long slices as we could manage. It was, for me, a kind of paradise—the kind of thing the breakfast tables at home didn't offer.

At home, we have often settled for a bit of hastily eaten non-artisanal toast and the kind of coffee we'd be a little embarrassed to serve you if you come over. I think we are laboring under the idea that bread is bad and health is suffering, which seems to be the North American way of things, at least on the west coast. We are inundated with messaging that whispers into our ears that bread and/or gluten is the reason we are unhappy or not thin enough.

In Friesland, I really liked coming down to breakfast and choosing from half a dozen types of bread and a rainbow of bread toppings. The Dutch have a lot of good stuff figured out. In Haarlem, we ate ontbijtkoek, a sort of dry, spicy soda bread, somewhere between a rye sandwich loaf and a gingerbread, slathered with naturally yellow, deeply flavorful butter. It was not too sweet—almost a savory cake—and it was sturdy enough to cut into slices and eat with your hands. In Amsterdam, every block seemed to have a bar with a sign outside advertising "koffie en gebak," with a chalk drawing of a towering pastry, usually apple pie (with whipped cream) and coffee, an ideal breakfast if there ever was one.

I think I would be a nicer person if I could roll out of bed in the morning and eat pie. For a few weeks, while testing recipes for this book, I did eat an inordinate amount of pie (I want to tell you that it took me weeks to get the pie recipes right—it didn't, really—but I lied and kept pie-making and ate every bit of it). I was—dare I say?—merry. I was *nice* before 9:00 a.m. And I know this evidence is only anecdotal, but it's compelling enough that I think we should all put down our smoothie bowls and our chia seeds and embrace Dutch breakfasts, sugar and white flour and cheese and all, because I think that is the way to a happier life. We can do better. We must do better. And while we're all thinking about how, let's share a few slices of white bread and a jar of Nutella. You make the coffee, and I'll set the table. I promise to be nice.

Hangop with Roasted Rhubarb

Hangop is made from strained yogurt—you can serve it plain, but I like to whisk a bit of orange juice and honey into it—and is good as a decadent breakfast or a low-key dessert. Avoid Greek yogurt, and choose a natural Balkan-style with between 3 and 6 percent fat and no starches or other thickeners. *Note*: Hangop can be made up to 48 hours in advance.

1 recipe hangop (p. 248)

1 large navel orange

2 tbsp honey

1 vanilla bean, scraped, or 1 tsp pure vanilla extract

1 lb (250 g) fresh rhubarb, trimmed

1 tbsp butter, melted

⅓ cup (75 g) granulated sugar

Spoon hangop into a bowl. Using a microplane or the small teeth on your cheese grater, zest entire orange into hangop. Squeeze orange into a small glass to juice; add 3 tbsp to yogurt and reserve remainder of juice for another use.

Add honey and vanilla and whisk mixture together until smooth. Store in a sealed container in refrigerator.

Preheat oven to 400°F (200°C).

Cut rhubarb into 2-in (5-cm) pieces. Place in small casserole or other baking dish, then add butter and sugar, and toss to coat.

Roast, uncovered, for 15–20 minutes, until liquid bubbles up and rhubarb is tender. Let cool to room temperature.

Spoon dollops of hangop into 4 bowls or onto rusks, then top with cooled rhubarb; drizzle lightly with rhubarb juice from baking dish.

Rice Pancakes

My son Hunter would live entirely on pancakes alone if I didn't occasionally intervene, and these are high on his list of favorites. They're little like silver dollar pancakes, and leavened with egg whites so they're light and airy and taste like rice pudding. Because they use leftover cooked rice they're the perfect breakfast for a lazy Saturday morning (or the perfect breakfast-for-dinner on some rainy Thursday). Hunter takes his with Nutella, but I like mine with a bit of warm applesauce.

2 eggs, yolks and whites
   separated

2 tbsp granulated sugar

1 tsp vanilla

2 cups (500 mL) plain cooked
   rice

½ cup (125 mL) all-purpose
   flour

½ cup (125 mL) whole milk

2 tbsp butter

In a large bowl, combine egg yolks, sugar, vanilla, rice, flour, and milk. Whisk to form a batter. Set aside.

In another bowl, whisk egg whites until they form stiff peaks. Fold egg whites into batter.

In a pan on medium-high heat, melt butter in batches, 2 tsp at a time, until all pancakes are cooked.

Drop 1 tbsp batter into pan and cook until bubbles form on top of each pancake; flip, and cook until golden, 1 to 2 minutes.

Currant Bread

···················· MAKES 1 LOAF ····················

Currant bread makes an excellent breakfast, and I recommend serving it toasted with butter and honey or apricot jam and a very strong cup of black tea. If you end up with stale leftovers, this makes fantastic French toast or bread pudding—use immediately or store in the freezer until you're ready to live your life right.

1 cup (250 mL) whole milk

pinch saffron or saffron extract (p. 19)

3 tbsp + 1 tsp honey, divided

1 tsp dry yeast

1 egg + 1 egg yolk, divided

1 large navel orange, zest and juice

3 tbsp neutral oil, such as canola

½ tsp kosher salt

1½ cups (375 mL) dried currants

3 cups (750 mL) all-purpose flour

In a pot on medium heat, warm milk with crumbled saffron threads to lukewarm, about 100°F (38°C). Remove from heat, and whisk in 3 tbsp honey and yeast. Set aside for about 5 minutes, until yeast is fluffy.

Pour milk into bowl and whisk to combine thoroughly with egg, orange zest and juice, oil, and salt.

Add currants and flour, and with wet hands knead to form a shaggy dough. Knead for about 8 minutes, or until dough is elastic. Form dough into a ball and place in a lightly oiled bowl. Cover with plastic wrap and a kitchen towel and let rest in a warm spot for about 40 minutes, or until nearly doubled in size.

Grease a 9 x 5-in (23 x 13-cm) loaf pan. Fit dough into prepared loaf pan. Once again, cover with plastic wrap and kitchen towel and leave in a warm place to rest for about 40 minutes.

Preheat oven to 325°F (165°C).

In a small bowl, mix egg yolk and remainder of honey with 1 tbsp water. Brush mixture over top of risen dough.

Bake for 35–40 minutes, until golden. Let sit in pan for 5 minutes before turning out onto a wire rack to cool completely. Wait until bread is completely cool before cutting a slice; if you want warm currant bread, reheat it or toast it after it has totally cooled.

Breakfast Bread

·········· MAKES 1 LOAF ··········

This is ontbijtkoek (gingerbread) that you should eat fresh and warm with butter and honey. The rye flour makes it more substantial than a typical loaf cake, and the molasses means it's not as sweet. It's virtuous cake, if there's such a thing, meant to be eaten in the morning. I like mine with a big mug of coffee with milk.

1 cup (250 mL) whole milk

¾ cup (175 mL) fancy molasses

1 egg

1 cup (250 mL) all-purpose flour

1 cup (250 mL) dark rye flour

1 tsp baking soda

½ tsp kosher salt

2 tsp ground ginger

1 tsp ground cinnamon

½ tsp ground allspice

½ tsp ground nutmeg

¼ tsp ground cloves

Preheat oven to 350°F (175°C). Grease a 9 x 5-in (23 x 13-cm) loaf pan, and set aside.

In a bowl, whisk together milk, molasses, and egg. Set aside.

In a large bowl, combine all-purpose and rye flour, baking soda, salt, ginger, cinnamon, allspice, nutmeg, and cloves.

Gently work wet ingredients into flour mixture until dry ingredients are just moistened but not lumpy.

Spoon batter into prepared loaf pan and bake for 45–50 minutes, or until a toothpick inserted into center of loaf comes out clean.

Turn out onto a wire rack to cool. For softer breakfast bread, wrap loaf tightly in plastic wrap after first 10 minutes of cooling.

Sugar Bread

In Drachten, we visited Boonstra Banketbakkerij en Chocolaterie for a loaf of royal family-approved sugar bread. Suikerbrood is a specialty of Friesland but is popular all over the country; it's best with a generous smear of good quality butter. If you cannot find pearl sugar, substitute gently crushed sugar cubes.

1 cup (250 mL) lukewarm whole milk

2 tbsp granulated sugar

½ tsp dry yeast

6 tbsp melted butter, divided

2 eggs, beaten

3½ cups (875 mL) all-purpose flour

1 tsp kosher salt

½ tsp cinnamon

½ tsp chopped dried ginger

4 oz (115 g) pearl sugar

In a large bowl, combine milk, granulated sugar, and yeast. Let stand until yeast is fluffy, about 5 minutes. Whisk in 3 tbsp melted butter and beaten eggs.

Add flour, salt, cinnamon, and dried ginger. Turn out onto a floured surface and knead until dough is smooth and elastic, between 8–10 minutes. Form dough into a ball and place in a lightly oiled bowl. Cover with plastic wrap and a clean kitchen towel, and let rise in a warm place until doubled in bulk, about 1 hour.

Preheat oven to 350°F (175°C). Grease a 9 x 5-in (23 x 13-cm) loaf pan and set aside.

Lightly flour a clean surface. Gently stretch dough out until it is about 9 in (22 cm) across and 12 in (30 cm) long. Paint dough with 2 tbsp melted butter, then sprinkle pearl sugar over top.

Gently but firmly roll dough from top, working to keep roll as tight as possible without squeezing too hard. Turn seam-side down, tuck ends underneath, and place in prepared loaf pan. Cover, and let rest for 40 minutes.

Uncover, and paint roll with remainder of melted butter. Bake for 30 minutes, until golden and fragrant. Let cool in the pan for 5 minutes, then turn onto a wire rack to completely cool. Cut into thick slices and serve.

Buttermilk Rye Waffles

MAKES 4 SERVINGS

A sturdy waffle is a great way to start your morning, and these are hearty and not too sweet. I like to make a big batch and provide a variety of topping options so guests can customize their own— Hunter's favorite way to eat these is topped with a bit of Nutella, a sliced banana, and a big foof of whipped cream. To make Nick's waffles diabetes-friendly, I top his with sambal oelek, sliced avocado, and a fried egg. For a fancy breakfast, serve with Apple-Raisin Compote (p. 46).

1 cup (250 mL) dark rye flour

1 cup (250 mL) all-purpose
    flour

2 tsp baking powder

½ tsp kosher salt

½ tsp ground nutmeg

2 cups buttermilk

2 eggs

3 tbsp molasses

¼ cup (60 mL) melted butter

Preheat waffle maker according to manufacturer's instructions.

In a large bowl, combine flours, baking powder, salt, and nutmeg.

In another bowl, whisk buttermilk, eggs, molasses, and butter until thoroughly combined. Stir dry ingredients into wet ingredients.

Cook in waffle maker according to manufacturer's instructions.

Applesauce Raisin Cake

MAKES 1 12-CUP (3-L) BUNDT CAKE

This cake is moist and sturdy, the kind of thing you can eat with your hands while telling an elaborate story to your best friends over coffee. You might serve it with butter and a bit of maple syrup or stroop, if you feel like dirtying a fork and plate; I like it on its own after I've picked all the raisins out. Let it cool completely before warming again to serve.

Tip: Drain and pat dry Brandied Raisins (p. 227), to use in this cake for a luxurious winter breakfast.

1 cup (250 mL) granulated sugar

2 eggs, beaten

1 cup (250 mL) unsweetened or homemade applesauce

1 cup (250 mL) buttermilk

2 tbsp melted butter

2 cups (500 mL) all-purpose flour

1 tsp baking soda

1 tsp ground cinnamon

½ tsp ground nutmeg

½ tsp kosher salt

1 cup (250 mL) raisins

2 tbsp confectioner's sugar

Preheat oven to 325°F (160°C).

Grease a Bundt pan and set aside.

In a large bowl, beat together sugar, eggs, applesauce, buttermilk, and melted butter.

In a separate bowl, whisk together flour, baking soda, cinnamon, nutmeg, and salt.

Fold dry ingredients into wet ingredients and stir until just moistened. Fold in raisins.

Spoon cake batter into prepared Bundt pan and spread to ensure mixture is distributed evenly.

Bake for 40–45 minutes, until a toothpick inserted into the deepest section of cake comes out clean.

Cool in pan for 10 minutes, then turn out onto a wire rack to cool completely.

Place confectioner's sugar in a fine-mesh sieve and shake over cake to dust.

Saffron Milk

Saffron milk is an old Dutch remedy for a cold, perhaps inspired by Ayurvedic medicine, dating from the time when Dutch merchants traded in India, where they had outposts for more than 200 years. It is soothing and mild, and I find it a nice way to start the day when one has accidentally woken up much too early.

1½ cups (375 mL) whole milk
1 tsp honey
pinch saffron or 2 tsp saffron extract (page 19)

In a pot on medium heat, warm milk, honey, and saffron until mixture just comes to a boil, about 7 minutes, whisking constantly. Watch pot, and if milk becomes frothy and attempts to boil over, remove from heat.

Pour into tea cups or a mug and serve hot.

Star Anise Milk

Star anise, a licorice-flavored spice from Southeast Asia, is thought to be beneficial for digestion (reduces bloating, stomach pain, and, um, flatulence), which makes this a nice accompaniment to a morning plate of bread and cheese. Try it—it's delicious!

1½ cups (375 mL) whole milk
1 tsp molasses
2 whole star anise

In a pot on medium heat, warm milk, molasses, and star anise until mixture just comes to a boil, about 7 minutes, whisking constantly. If the milk becomes frothy and attempts to boil over, remove from heat. Pour into teacups or a mug and serve hot.

Sweet Gerties

This simple pancake dish is inspired by the recipe for "Deuse Geertjes" in Peter Rose's translation of *The Sensible Cook: Dutch Foodways in the Old and the New World.* Sweet with rose water and cinnamon, gerties are meant to be fried in butter quickly, as "otherwise they would fall." Given that height—or at least airiness—is the goal, I've reimagined these as individual Dutch Babies. Leave the batter out overnight before cooking for best results. Serve with syrup or jam, or sweetened yogurt and fresh berries.

1 cup (250 mL) whole milk

4 eggs

2 tbsp melted butter

2 tbsp granulated sugar

1 tbsp rose water

½ tsp ground cinnamon

½ tsp kosher salt

1 cup (250 mL) all-purpose
    flour

6 tbsp room-temperature butter

In a large bowl, whisk all ingredients—except 6 tbsp butter—together and let stand for at least 1 and up to 24 hours before cooking.

Place six 6-oz (17-mL) ramekins on a baking sheet in a cold oven, and preheat oven to 425°F (218°C).

When oven is heated to temperature, remove pan and put 1 tbsp butter in each ramekin. Let butter melt, about 30 seconds, then divide batter evenly between ramekins.

Bake for 15–20 minutes, until puffed and golden. Check on them through the oven window—opening the oven will cause the Sweet Gerties to fall.

Serve hot, right from the oven.

Apple-Raisin Compote

This recipe is infinitely adaptable. I often substitute dried cranberries for the raisins and double the batch for company.

2 tbsp butter

2 tbsp brown sugar

1 lb (454 g) tart apples, such as Granny Smith, peeled and diced

½ cup (125 mL) raisins

1 tsp vanilla extract

¼ tsp cinnamon

In a small saucepan on medium-high heat, melt butter and brown sugar. Add apples, and cook for about 2 minutes. Add raisins, vanilla, and cinnamon, and cook for another 2–4 minutes, until liquid is syrupy, raisins have plumped, and apples have softened.

Serve warm over waffles (p. 40) or pannekoeken (p. 107).

Oatmeal with Dried Fruit & Almonds

······· · MAKES 4 SERVINGS · ·······

I married the kind of person who needs something like 10 hours of sleep to function; our son, also a monster, needs 12. I usually get 6 or 7, so some mornings, when I'm feeling kindly toward them, I'll whip up a pot of this oatmeal, and it fills us all up and reduces our morning crankies. The dried fruit makes it feel a little fancy; use raisins if you prefer, but I love dried cranberries with this.

½ cup (125 mL) slivered almonds
4 oz (115 g) dried apricots
½ cup (125 mL) dried cranberries
½ cup (125 mL) orange juice
4 tbsp honey, divided
¼ tsp ground cinnamon
3 cups (750 mL) whole milk
1⅓ cups (315 mL) large-flake rolled oats
¼ tsp ground nutmeg
pinch of salt

Preheat oven to 350°F (180°C). Spread almonds in a single layer in a pie plate or on a baking sheet.

In a small saucepan on medium heat, add apricots, cranberries, orange juice, 2 tbsp honey, and cinnamon, plus ½ cup (125 mL) water. Bring to a gentle simmer. Cook until most of the liquid is absorbed by fruit, about 20 minutes.

Toast almonds for about 4 minutes, until golden. Remove from oven and set aside.

Meanwhile, fill a second saucepan with milk and remainder of honey, and on medium-high heat, bring to a gentle boil. Reduce heat to medium, and stir in oats, nutmeg, and salt. Cook, stirring frequently, for about 10 minutes, or until creamy. Let oats rest for 5 minutes before serving.

Spoon into 4 bowls, and top with plumped fruit and toasted almonds.

Eggs in Dutch Lettuce

MAKES 4–6 SERVINGS

"Lettuce" is maybe a loose term here. The point is to use up your greens, whether that means lettuce or whatever else is in season (or going nuts in the garden). I prefer a mix of curly endive, escarole, watercress, Lacinato kale, spinach, or green leaf lettuce, but use what you have. I like it as much for dinner as for breakfast. Serve with crusty bread and hot sauce.

2 lb (900 g) mixed leafy greens, roughly chopped

¼ cup (60 g) butter

2 leeks, white and light-green parts only, thinly sliced

3 garlic cloves, minced

1 tsp grainy Dijon mustard

1 tsp kosher salt

2 tbsp all-purpose flour

½ cup (125 mL) dry white wine

1 cup (250 mL) whole milk

½ cup (125 mL) heavy cream

¼ tsp ground black pepper

¼ tsp ground nutmeg

3.5 oz (100 g) shredded Gouda

6 eggs

kosher salt, to taste

3 tbsp chopped fresh basil

1 scallion, minced

Preheat oven to 375°F (190°C).

Fill a large bowl with cold water and ice cubes. Set aside.

On high heat, bring a large pot of salted water to a rolling boil. Add greens, and boil for 30–60 seconds, until greens have brightened in color and wilted. Strain greens into a colander, then place in bowl with cold water and ice. Set aside.

In a large pan on medium heat, melt butter and add leeks. Sauté until leeks have softened, about 4 minutes. Add garlic, and sauté for 1 minute. Stir in mustard, salt, and flour.

Drain cooled greens, and squeeze to release water. Place greens in a clean dishtowel and wring out any remaining liquid.

Add wine, and cook until liquid has reduced slightly, about 3 minutes. Add greens and milk, and simmer until milk begins to thicken and greens soften further, another 3–5 minutes.

Stir in cream, pepper, nutmeg, and Gouda, then remove pan from heat. Make 6 little wells in greens mixture. Crack an egg into each well. Sprinkle eggs with a pinch of kosher salt.

Bake until egg whites are just set, 10–12 minutes. For hard yolks, bake for 20 minutes (but I want you to know that I do not approve).

Before serving, sprinkle basil and scallions over eggs.

COFFEE TIME & DAYTIME ENTERTAINING

COFFEE TIME & DAYTIME ENTERTAINING

We stayed with Nick's family in Friesland, the northern province of the Netherlands, for a weekend. They live in a neat, very pretty village of maybe 150 people; it's a beautiful place, with fields dotted with sheep, and even in winter it is somehow still very green. There was a community center, a bank, a Michelin-starred restaurant, and a "patat," a spot that was lit like a deli and strewn with older men watching soccer games like a local pub, and where you could buy any number of deep-fried delicacies, from friet (fries) to kroketten to frikandel, which is like a hot dog, but with no casing. The landscape—mostly flat, with misty green fields and fruit trees and the occasional black-and-white Holstein Friesian—reminded me very much of Ladner, a small suburb of Vancouver, British Columbia, where many Dutch people settled on immigrating to Canada, as well as Lynden, a small town in Washington state that is also very, very Dutch.

Dutch identity is complex, and northerners are sometimes viewed as idiosyncratic, perhaps for their strong opinions or tendency to see themselves as culturally distinct—they maintain their own language, though they also speak Dutch. Think of the relationship between Scotland and England in terms of how Frisians view themselves in comparison to the Netherlands. If you've ever mistakenly called a Scottish person English, you will know what I mean.

(As an aside, they are also tall—poetically tall—and historically, they are the tallest people in Europe. In *Inferno*, the 14th-century poet Dante describes the height of a demon as so big that "not even three tall Frieslanders, were they set one upon the other, would have matched his height." I am not sure how I feel knowing that I will eventually have to feed a teenage boy with Frisian genes.)

(Reluctant. I feel reluctant.)

The Frisians are also known for their generous hospitality. And nowhere is this more apparent than when it is time for coffee—and it is often time for coffee. Our host was so serious about coffee that it seemed to delight him to prepare it, over and over again, for each individual guest in his kitchen. And so, at breakfast and midday and in the late afternoon (we had to decline the evening coffee, because we are weak and cannot sleep having had caffeine after a certain hour), we sat and sipped little cups of strong coffee with cream and ate crisp, spicy cookies at his table, and at his favorite little café, and it was everything I imagine North American coffee culture aspires to, but with the effortlessness of expertise and none of the fuss. Simple. Perfect. And always with a little something sweet to go with.

You don't see people wandering the streets of the cities in the Netherlands with big paper cups in hand—this was only an option at Starbucks (we only went twice, and were embarrassed about it). And the only people at Starbucks seemed to be Nick and I and an assortment of British tourists. Everywhere else, the cafés served strong little cups of thick, aromatic black coffee, the sort of thing designed to be lingered over and not quaffed as if out of a jug (which is how I prefer mine, but I will admit, I have no class). Coffee is serious, and coffee time is serious. It is a seated affair.

And that is fine too, because if there is one thing the Dutch take more seriously than sitting down for coffee, it's sweets. The Dutch sweet tooth is unparalleled, and their pastries are hearty and seem to have been designed explicitly to pair with a strong, dark brew.

My first introduction to the heartiness of Dutch pastries was my mother-in-law's boeter-koek, or butter cake, a dense, almond-scented cake that is somewhere between shortbread and a brownie, texture-wise, and perfect with a cup of black tea. I appreciate that Dutch bakers seem to understand dunkability—a pastry must have the structural integrity to withstand a bit of dipping in hot liquid, because that is inevitable. I cannot abide a cookie that dissolves in my drink, and it seems the Dutch can't either.

Sitting down to coffee or tea in the late afternoon, after work, is not something I have been able to easily incorporate into my daily life, but at the office, I have taken to pausing for coffee with some of the other women in the morning, and sharing a sweet bite then. We have a table in the middle of the office, and we all slouch around it every morning, sipping our *déclassé* mug coffee and sharing muffins or cookies or whatever cake I have kicking around from the weekend. The result is that we are not just co-workers, but work family, and we are very unprofessional but also very close now. This, I think, is the benefit to kof-feetijd, or coffee time; it is not just about sweets and caffeine, but about sharing a moment with the people around you.

While sipping coffee or tea and a little something sweet in the late afternoon (or disrupting everyone else in the office with your loud mid-morning chatter) may not be something easily incorporated into your daily life, many of the recipes that follow are very weekend-friendly, the kind of thing you could make and take to a wedding or baby shower or serve to guests who pop by on Sunday afternoon. Most of them are, by their nature, the kind of thing that will hold for a couple of days, so you can make them during the week and save them for when you need them; my mother-in-law makes a couple of butter cakes at a time and then freezes them for evening meetings and weekend get-togethers.

I think the Friese have the right idea. You should take as many moments as you need to sit and sip something you love, whether that's expertly brewed coffee or your favorite tea or even a big bucket of watery North American coffee. And you should have a cookie or a piece of cake, and you should have strong opinions that you don't mind sharing, and you should open your home to whomever needs a bit of warmth or a little break or a bit of ritual. Whether you are Friese or not, more of this is good for us all.

Frisian Thumb Cookies

These are maybe supposed to be thumb-shaped, or maybe supposed to feature the thumbprint of their baker, but either way they are delicious. We stepped inside from the bracing cold one January afternoon in the northern town of Dokkum, and these little cookies—called dumkes—and the creamy latte they accompanied were exactly what we needed.

½ cup (125 mL) slivered almonds

½ cup whole hazelnuts

1 tbsp fennel seeds

½ lb (250 g) room-temperature butter

½ cup (125 mL) brown sugar

½ cup (125 mL) granulated sugar

1 egg

1 tsp anise extract

¼ tsp ground cinnamon

¼ tsp kosher salt

2 cups (500 mL) all-purpose flour

1 tsp baking powder

1 tsp baking soda

Preheat oven to 400°F (200°C).

Place almonds, hazelnuts, and fennel seeds in a baking dish, and toast in oven for 7 minutes. Toss nut mixture, then toast for an additional 5–7 minutes, until golden and fragrant. Set aside to cool.

In a large bowl, cream butter, brown sugar, and granulated sugar together until fluffy. Scrape down sides of bowl with a spatula, then add egg, anise extract, cinnamon, and salt, and mix to combine thoroughly.

When cool enough to handle, transfer nut mixture to a cutting board and finely chop. Add chopped nuts to butter mixture, and beat to combine.

In a separate bowl, whisk together flour, baking powder, and baking soda. Stir flour mixture into butter mixture, and combine to form a dough.

Place dough on a sheet of plastic wrap, then seal. Refrigerate for 15 minutes.

Preheat oven to 375°F (190°C).

Roll out chilled dough to about 10 x 14-in (25 x 36-cm). Cutting lengthwise, create 8 long slices. Cut 6 times crosswise to create 48 roughly equal-sized pieces.

Frisian Thumb Cookies cont'd

Working in batches, place cookies on a baking sheet and bake 12–14 minutes or until lightly golden around edges. Cool completely on a wire rack, then serve with coffee. Will keep frozen in an airtight container for up to 3 months.

Beppe's Butter Cake

MAKES 8 SERVINGS

The VanderWoud family boeterkoek (butter cake) comes from Nick's Beppe. (Beppe is Frisian for "grandmother.") This almond-flavored cake—with a texture somewhere between shortbread and a brownie—is the dish I most associate with Nick's family. Now that Beppe is in her eighties and doesn't bake much anymore, Nick's mom brings butter cakes to them every week for Pake (Nick's grandfather) and Beppe to share.

Tip: If you prefer your butter cake to be firmer and more cookie-like, make the recipe as described below but bake in a 9-in (23-cm) round pan, and reduce baking time to 25–30 minutes.

½ cup (125 mL) butter

1 cup (250 mL) + 1 tbsp granulated sugar, divided

1 tsp almond extract

2 eggs, divided

½ tsp kosher salt

1¼ (310 mL) cups all-purpose flour

1 tsp baking powder

½ cup (125 mL) slivered almonds

Preheat oven to 325°F (160°C). Grease an 8-in (20-cm) round cake pan, and line bottom with parchment paper.

In a large bowl, beat together butter and 1 cup sugar. Beat in almond extract, 1 egg, 1 egg yolk, and salt. Scrape sides of bowl down and beat until fluffy. Set aside 1 egg white.

In a separate bowl, whisk together flour and baking powder.

Add dry ingredients to wet ingredients, and mix until just combined. Spoon mixture into prepared pan. Wet hands with cold water, and gently press dough to spread evenly around cake pan.

In a bowl, whisk reserved egg white until frothy, and pour over cake. Gently brush to spread evenly. Scatter almonds over top, then sprinkle evenly with 1 tbsp sugar.

Bake for 35–40 minutes, until golden. Cool for 10 minutes in pan, then gently turn out onto a wire rack—almond side up—to cool completely.

Cut into wedges to serve.

Saffron Butter Cake

This is a riff on Beppe's recipe—because Nick doesn't like almond flavoring or appreciate the butter cake of his people. We all know he is wrong. Lightly saffron-flavored and studded with chopped pistachios, this cake goes beautifully with a glass of prosecco—serve it with brunch.

Tip: **If you prefer a firmer, more cookie-like butter cake, make the recipe as described below but bake in a 9-in (23-cm) round pan, and reduce baking time to 25–30 minutes.**

½ cup (125mL) butter

1 cup (250mL) + 1 tbsp granulated sugar, divided

saffron extract: pinch saffron, steeped in 2 tbsp boiling water for 10 minutes

½ tsp vanilla extract

2 eggs, divided

½ tsp kosher salt

1¼ (310 mL) cups all-purpose flour

1 tsp baking powder

½ cup (125 mL) shelled pistachios, roughly chopped

Preheat oven to 325°F (160°C). Grease an 8-in (20-cm) round cake pan, and line bottom with parchment paper.

In a bowl, beat together butter and sugar. Beat in 1 tbsp saffron extract, vanilla extract, 1 egg, 1 egg yolk, and salt. Scrape sides of bowl down and beat until fluffy. Set aside 1 egg white.

In a separate bowl, whisk together flour and baking powder.

Add dry ingredients to wet ingredients, and mix until just combined. Spoon mixture into prepared pan. Wet hands with cold water, and gently press dough to spread evenly around cake pan.

In a bowl, whisk reserved egg white with remainder of saffron extract until frothy, and pour over cake. Gently brush mixture to spread evenly. Scatter pistachios over top, then sprinkle evenly with remaining 1 tbsp sugar.

Bake for 35–40 minutes, until golden. Cool for 10 minutes in pan, then gently turn out onto a wire rack—pistachio side up—to cool completely.

Cut into wedges to serve.

Apricot & Buttermilk Coffee Cake

I will admit to having had this cake for breakfast on more than one occasion—it goes very nicely with Saffron Milk (p. 44) and a dollop of vanilla yogurt to stand in for whipped cream. As upside-down cakes go, it's fairly simple to prepare, and it looks pretty on a cake stand if you're entertaining guests in the afternoon.

5 oz (125 g) dried apricots

½ cup (125 mL) apricot jam

½ cup (125 mL) room-temperature butter

1 cup (250 mL) granulated sugar

2 eggs

1 tsp vanilla extract

1 lemon, zested and juiced

¼ tsp kosher salt

1 cup (250 mL) buttermilk

2 cups (500 mL) all-purpose flour

½ tsp baking powder

½ tsp baking soda

Preheat oven to 350°F (175°C). Grease a 9-in (23-cm) round cake pan, and line bottom with parchment paper.

Place dried apricots in bowl and cover with boiling water. Let soak until cool enough to handle, about 15 minutes. With your fingers, pull each apricot in halve lengthwise along the seam. Place apricot halves around bottom of prepared pan, split-side up. Spoon jam over apricots. Set aside.

In a bowl, beat together butter and sugar. Beat in eggs until light and fluffy.

Whisk in vanilla, lemon zest and juice, salt, and buttermilk.

In a separate bowl, mix together flour, baking powder, and baking soda. Add dry ingredients to wet ingredients and beat until dry ingredients are just moistened but no lumps remain.

Spoon batter over prepared apricots, and bake for 40–45 minutes, until golden and a toothpick inserted into center comes out clean. Cool in pan for 5 minutes, then turn out onto a wire rack to cool completely.

Limburg Tart

Limburg tarts are tarts with thin, bread-like crusts gently leavened with a small amount of yeast. The secret is to not develop a lot of gluten—mix the wet and dry ingredients just enough to form a dough; you do not want to overmix this. Some Limburg-style tarts have fruit baked into the custard. My preference (for most reliable results) is to top the edges of the tart with fresh fruit—and a heap of whipped cream in the middle—after the tart has baked and cooled. Use what's in season—I like fresh blackberries best.

CRUST

¼ cup (60 mL) whole milk, lukewarm

½ tsp dry yeast

1 tbsp granulated sugar

welted butter

1 egg, beaten

¼ tsp kosher salt

1¼ cups (310 mL) all-purpose flour

FILLING

6 egg yolks, beaten

1 tsp vanilla extract

1 ½ cups (375 mL) whole milk

½ cup (125 mL) heavy cream

⅓ cup (80 mL) granulated sugar

1 tbsp butter

TOPPING

1 cup (250 mL) whipping cream (optional)

1 tbsp sugar

2 cups (500 mL) sliced fresh fruit or whole berries

To prepare crust: In a large mixing bowl, combine gently warmed milk, yeast, and sugar. Let stand for about 5 minutes, until yeast begins to foam and appear fluffy. Whisk in melted butter, egg, salt, and flour, and knead just to form a ball. Press dough into a disk-shape and let rest in same bowl, covered with plastic wrap and a clean kitchen towel, for about 40 minutes.

Preheat oven to 400°F (200°C).

Grease a 9 1/2-in (24-cm) tart pan with a removable bottom. Lightly flour a clean surface, and roll out dough to about 11 in (28 cm) in diameter. Drape dough over prepared tart pan, gently pressing down and into ridges around pan. Run a rolling pin or sharp knife around top of tart pan to neatly trim off excess dough.

To make filling: In a large bowl, beat together egg yolks and vanilla until smooth.

In a pot on medium-high, heat milk, cream, and sugar, and bring to a boil. Remove immediately from heat. Whisking constantly, pour milk mixture in a thin stream into egg yolks. Pour back into pot and return to heat, still whisking constantly, until it thickens, about 4 minutes. Pour through a fine-mesh sieve into prepared crust.

Limburg Tart cont'd

Bake for 25–30 minutes, until crust is golden-brown and has pulled away from edges of pan. The custard will not appear completely set in the middle, but it will set as it cools. Let cool in pan for 10 minutes, then remove to a wire rack and cool to room temperature.

In a bowl, whip cream with sugar until it reaches desired consistency. Top tart with sliced fresh fruit and whipped cream and serve at room temperature, or refrigerate without whipped cream until ready to serve.

Prune Tart

Prunes and other dried fruits feature prominently in Dutch cuisine, and in some cases there are historic reasons for this; in the 18th century, prunes—dried plums—were thought to be healthier than fresh plums. Which is just as well, as plum season is short and you can have this spicy prune pie any time of year. The filling is reminiscent of English mincemeat, making this a festive tart for fall and early winter.

FILLING

10.5 oz (300 g) pitted prunes, roughly chopped

1 cup (250 mL) unsweetened or homemade applesauce

¾ cup (175 mL) packed brown sugar

½ cup (125 mL) brandy

1½ tsp ground ginger

½ tsp ground cinnamon

¼ tsp ground allspice

CRUST

¼ cup (60 mL) whole milk, lukewarm

½ tsp dry yeast

1 tbsp granulated sugar

2 tbsp melted butter

1 egg, beaten

¼ tsp kosher salt

1¼ cups (310 mL) all-purpose flour

In a bowl, cover prunes with 2 cups (500 mL) boiling water. Let stand for at least 2 and up to 12 hours.

Pour prune and water mixture into saucepan on medium heat, and add applesauce, brown sugar, brandy, ginger, cinnamon, and allspice. Stew until thick and jammy, about 40 minutes, or until it reaches about 220°F (105°C). Stir regularly to prevent scorching.

Meanwhile, make the crust. In a large mixing bowl, combine gently warmed milk, yeast, and sugar. Let stand for about 5 minutes, until the yeast begins to foam and look fluffy. Whisk in melted butter, egg, salt, and flour, and knead just enough to form a ball. Press dough into a disk-shape and let rest in same bowl, covered with plastic wrap and a clean kitchen towel, for about 40 minutes.

Grease a 9.5-in (24-cm) tart pan with a removable bottom. Preheat oven to 400°F (200°C).

Lightly flour a clean surface, and roll dough out to about 11 in (28 cm) in diameter. Drape dough over prepared tart pan, gently pressing down and into ridges around pan. Run a rolling pin or sharp knife around top of pan to neatly trim off excess dough. Using a fork, prick holes in base of crust every inch (2.5 cm) or so.

Pour prune mixture into crust. Bake for 25–30 minutes, until crust is golden-brown and has pulled away from edges of pan. Let cool in the pan for 10 minutes, then cool to room temperature on a wire rack.

Serve at room temperature.

Rice Tart

This is a Limburg-style tart, a thin, bread-like crust suspending a thin layer of rice pudding. Limburg tarts—called vlaai—are generally flat; I suspect the end-goal is a sturdy pie with enough surface area to support a generous floof of whipped cream. Because this is not exactly dessert, it's less sweet than you might expect. Either top it with whipped cream and shaved chocolate and serve it right away, or make ahead and top individual slices with whipped cream to serve. If you are not in the mood to whip cream, this is also nice with a little bit of raspberry jam.

CRUST

¼ cup (60 mL) whole milk, lukewarm

½ tsp dry yeast

1 tbsp granulated sugar

2 tbsp melted butter

1 egg, beaten

¼ tsp kosher salt

1¼ cups (310 mL) all-purpose flour

FILLING

¼ cup (60 mL) uncooked long-grain white rice

2 cups (500 mL) whole milk

⅓ cup (80 mL) granulated sugar

1 tbsp brandy

1 tbsp butter

½ cup (125 mL) cream

1 tsp vanilla extract

3 egg yolks, beaten

Topping

1 cup (250 mL) whipping cream (optional)

1 tbsp granulated sugar (optional)

1–2 tbsp chocolate shavings (optional)

In a large mixing bowl, combine gently warmed milk, yeast, and 1 tbsp sugar. Let stand for about 5 minutes, until the yeast begins to foam and appear fluffy. Whisk in melted butter, egg, salt, and flour, and knead just enough to form a ball. Press dough into a disk-shape and let rest in same bowl, covered with plastic wrap and a clean kitchen towel, for about 40 minutes.

Preheat oven to 400°F (200°C).

In a heavy-bottomed pan on medium-high heat, bring rice and 3/4 cup (175 mL) water to a boil. Cook, stirring occasionally, until rice has absorbed water, about 10 minutes. Add milk and sugar, and bring back to a gentle boil.

Simmer for about 20 minutes, until rice is tender and appears overdone, milk has reduced by about half, and mixture has thickened. For the first 10 minutes, stir frequently, then stir constantly so that mixture doesn't stick to pan. Add brandy and butter, and stir to combine.

Grease a 9 1/2-in (24-cm) tart pan with a removable bottom.

Lightly flour a clean surface, and roll dough out to about 11 in (28 cm) in diameter. Drape dough over prepared tart pan, gently pressing down and into ridges around pan. Run a rolling pin or sharp knife around top of pan to neatly trim off excess dough.

Rice Tart cont'd

Whisk cream and vanilla extract into rice mixture. Working quickly, drizzle egg yolks into rice mixture, whisking to combine.

Spoon mixture into pan, spreading with a spatula so that custard evenly fills the crust.

Bake for 25–30 minutes, until crust is golden-brown and has pulled away from edges of pan, and custard has set in the middle—give pan a little wiggle; it shouldn't slosh around. Let cool in pan for 10 minutes, then cool to room temperature on a wire rack.

In a bowl, beat whipping cream with sugar until it reaches desired consistency, then dollop over tart. Sprinkle tart with chocolate shavings, if desired.

Serve at room temperature, or refrigerate without whipped cream until ready to serve.

Apple Tart

Everywhere in Amsterdam, cafés have signs out front advertising a slice of apple pie—appeltaart—with whipped cream and coffee for breakfast or koffeetijd. The pies are tall, made in a springform pan, and the crust is sturdy and cookie-like. The filling is dense with thick-sliced apples and meant to be hearty and substantial. It's as good with hot coffee as it is with a cold glass of dark Belgian beer. Serve with whipped cream.

3½ cups (875 mL) all-purpose flour

¾ cup (375 mL) + 1 tbsp granulated sugar

1 tsp kosher salt, divided

½ tsp ground nutmeg

10 tbsp cold butter, in 1 tbsp pieces

¼ cup (60 mL) cold whole milk

1 egg, beaten

2 lb (900 g) tart green apples, such as Granny Smith

2 lb (900 g) sweet, firm apples, such as Ambrosia or Honeycrisp

1 cup (250 mL) brown sugar, packed

3 tbsp cornstarch

2 tbsp lemon juice

½ tsp vanilla extract

1 egg yolk

½ tsp ground cinnamon

Preheat oven to 325°F (160°C).

In a large bowl, combine flour, ¾ cup (175 mL) granulated sugar, salt, and nutmeg. Mix to combine well.

Using your fingers, crumble butter into bowl, squeezing bits of butter into flour to form a sandy, pebbly-looking mixture. Stir in milk and egg, then press dough into a ball and wrap tightly with plastic wrap. Refrigerate for 20 minutes.

Peel and core apples, then cut lengthwise into strips about ½ in (1 cm), then halve crosswise. Place apples in large bowl.

Add brown sugar, cornstarch, lemon juice, and vanilla extract, and mix thoroughly using your hands.

Grease a 9-in (23-cm) springform pan.

Cut off ⅓ of dough, and set aside. Roll out remainder of dough to about 16 in (40 cm) in diameter. Gently drape dough over prepared springform pan and gently nestle into pan, pressing on bottom and sides. If there are gaps, pinch off bits of overhanging dough to use as patches. Seal all cracks or holes in dough.

Pour apples into crust, gently pressing to fit. With a spatula, scrape remainder of liquid in bowl and drizzle over apples.

Apple Tart cont'd

Roll out remainder of dough to a diameter of about 11 in (27 cm) and cut into strips at least ½-in (1-cm) wide. Create a lattice by weaving strips about 1 in (2.5 cm) apart over top of pie. Pinch or press strips onto bottom crust, then run a sharp knife around outside to trim excess.

In a small bowl, whisk together egg yolk and 1 tbsp cold water. With a pastry brush, paint top crust of pie.

In another small bowl, combine remainder of sugar and cinnamon. With a fine-mesh strainer, shake mixture over top of pie.

Bake for 60–70 minutes, until bubbling, golden, and crisp. Let cool in pan. Release from pan and place on serving tray. Cut into slices and serve at room temperature.

Raisin Bars

Community cookbooks—especially by groups of church ladies—are about my favorite thing; you know the recipes will work and that families will like them and that people have asked for them. A tattered spiral-bound cookbook (typed on a typewriter!) from a Dutch church in Edmonton provided the basis for this recipe, which is like a date square but with raisins and orange juice instead. This is good with coffee, especially with a bit of Grand Marnier sneaked in while no one's looking.

13 oz (375 g) raisins

1¼ cups (310 mL) brown sugar, divided

2 tbsp cornstarch

2 cups (500 mL) orange juice

1 tsp vanilla extract

1 tsp ground cinnamon

½ tsp ground allspice

1½ cups (375 mL) rolled oats

1 cup (250 mL) all-purpose flour

½ cup (125 mL) dark rye flour

½ tsp kosher salt

¾ cup (175 mL) room-temperature butter

¼ cup (60 mL) whole milk

Preheat oven to 350°F (175°C). Grease an 8-in (20-cm) square baking dish, and line bottom with parchment paper.

In a saucepan, combine raisins with ½ cup (125 mL) brown sugar and cornstarch. Stir so that sugar mixture coats raisins. Add orange juice, then place pan on medium heat. Add vanilla extract, cinnamon, and allspice. Simmer for 5–10 minutes, or until thickened. Set aside.

In a large bowl, combine remainder of brown sugar with oats, flours, and salt. Using your hands, work butter into flour to form a sandy, pebbly-looking mixture. Stir in milk, then remove 1 cup (250 mL) of mixture and set aside.

Press oat mixture into bottom of prepared pan, then pour raisin mixture over top, spreading evenly across pan. Sprinkle reserved oat mixture evenly over top.

Bake for 30–35 minutes, until golden and bubbly around the edges. Cool in pan, then cut into squares or slices to serve.

Rose Meringues

This recipe exists almost entirely as an excuse to use up your spare egg whites. However, I can't stop eating them crumbled over a bit of yogurt with a dollop of rhubarb preserves (p. 243) for breakfast or dessert on the patio in late spring. Garnish with your favorite sprinkles and dye the hue of your choice (or not, if you prefer)—I like mine with two drops of red food coloring for peak rosiness.

4 egg whites, cold
½ tsp lemon juice
1 cup (250 mL) confectioner's
  sugar
1 tbsp rose water
2 drops food coloring (optional)
1 tsp rainbow or other sprinkles
  (optional)

Preheat oven to 350°F (175°C).

Line a baking sheet with parchment paper. Using a pencil, trace 12 circles onto paper, each about 3-in (7.5-cm) in diameter. Flip parchment over.

In a large bowl, beat egg whites with lemon juice until frothy and just beginning to look opaque, 2–3 minutes. Add ½ cup (125 mL) confectioner's sugar, beating continuously. Add rose water, and continue to beat. Add remainder of confectioner's sugar, and continue to beat until stiff peaks form, about 2–3 minutes. Egg mixture should appear glossy and white, and should hold its shape—peaks should not fall when shaken.

Beat in food coloring for 10 seconds, then spoon mixture onto circles on parchment paper, smoothing evenly to fill in. Dust lightly with sprinkles.

Place meringues in oven and immediately lower heat to 200°F (95°C). Bake for 75 minutes, until dry-looking but not browned or cracked. Do not open the door at any time. After 75 minutes, turn off oven and leave meringues inside to cool for at least 3 hours, preferably overnight.

Remove meringues and place in a sealed container. Store in a dry place for up to 3 days. Do not refrigerate.

Kandeel

Kandeel is mulled white wine thickened with egg yolks, typically served to celebrate the birth of a child; try it at the next baby shower. It's reminiscent of warm apple cider—look for an inexpensive German Riesling and you'll get those apple-like notes.

3 cups (750 mL) off-dry white wine, such as Riesling
1 cup (250 mL) granulated sugar
2 whole star anise
1 lemon, sliced into rounds
6 egg yolks
1 tsp vanilla extract
½ tsp ground cinnamon
6 cinnamon sticks

In a saucepan on medium heat, stir wine and sugar until sugar dissolves. Add star anise and lemon slices, and bring to a gentle simmer before reducing heat to low. Simmer gently for 30 minutes.

Meanwhile, whisk together egg yolks, vanilla extract, and ground cinnamon.

Place cinnamon sticks in 6 large wine glasses and set aside.

Remove lemon slices and star anise from wine, and remove from heat. Whisking constantly, pour half, in a thin stream, into egg-yolk mixture. Pour back into saucepan and return to stove, whisking constantly. Cook on low heat until mixture has thickened and is foamy, about 3 minutes.

Divide wine mixture evenly between wine glasses and drink warm.

BORRELS (DUTCH TAPAS)

TRADITIONAL BITTERBALLS
78

PAPRIKA BITTERBALLS
80

POTATO-KALE BITTERBALLS
82

GARLIC SHRIMP
86

MARINATED HERRING
89

CREAMED HERRING
90

CURRY CASHEWS
91

CHEESE COOKIES
92

FRIED CHEESE BALLS
94

CHEESE CIGARS
95

KIBBELING
96

DUTCH FRIES
98

HAIRDRESSER FRIES
99

UITSMIJTER
101

BORRELS (DUTCH TAPAS)

"The Dutch their wine, and all their brandy lose, Disarm'd of that from which their courage grows."
—*Instructions to a Painter...* by Edmund Waller, 1665

"In de wijn is de waarheid." (In wine there is truth.) —Dutch proverb (based on the Latin phrase)

We had arrived in the Netherlands in the afternoon after eleven hours of travel when the plans for our first-choice place to stay—a three-hour drive from Amsterdam—fell through. In an instant, we went from confident about the weeks ahead to terrified that we'd have to spend the night in the airport with our five-year-old (who hadn't slept on the plane), and also we were starving. I stress-barfed in a garbage can on the way to the bathroom where I intended to have a quick cry, and then we grabbed a beer and some fries with mayonnaise near the currency exchange and figured out our next move.

We ended up in Haarlem, in a townhouse right in the center of town and not too far from an Albert Heijn grocery store. And Hunter fell asleep.

He slept for hours, and we were so hungry. We thought we'd let him nap, but the thing about kids is that they will sleep only as much as they will sleep—they will not simply lay there patiently in the morning until you get up; no. They will find themselves rested at 4:00 a.m., even if you are jet-lagged, and want to be with you and talk to you—have a conversation with you—even if you feel like you are dying. So we woke him up after a couple of hours (he was not happy about it) and dragged his limp, heavy body to the supermarket to find something—anything—that would do for dinner and then breakfast the next day. He slept in the shopping cart while we beheld the borrels case, in all its wonder.

Borrels, or little snacky bites, are the Dutch way of pausing for a drink. You have a glass of wine or gin, or a beer, and you eat a bit of cheese, maybe some salumi or cold garlic shrimp or some deep-fried treats, and then you go about your day. Grocery stores offer small containers for all your borrels cravings—cheese wrapped in thinly sliced charcuterie; olives stuffed with garlic and marinated in vinegar and herbs; crisp crackers topped with shaved Gouda or oude Amsterdamse kaas (cheese); plastic tubs of filet Americain, a pâté of raw beef and spices topped with minced white onions; or rosettes of Spanish ham, two to a container, so expensive at home and so astonishingly cheap there. Bars and cafés offer bitterballen, like croquettes but smaller, a little ball of meat that's been breaded and fried so that it's simultaneously crunchy and oozy, or kibbeling, fried chunks of cod or other white fish with a sweet take on tartar sauce. The important thing is a drink and a snack, either right after work or in the evening, or in the afternoon on a weekend when you have nothing to do but find cold gin and a patio. I no longer have goals that do not involve snacks that go well with drinks.

You can have borrels alone—I have held private borreltijd (basically, happy hour) in the bathtub with some rosé, Fleetwood Mac, and spiced cashews—though these are best served with friends, either in a café or at home. And if you're breaking out the oil for deep-frying, it's best to do a large batch so you might as well invite company.

I'll admit that the busy pace of our lives in Vancouver is not really conducive to setting

Ease into your borrels.

aside a few minutes per day for a drink and a snack, but you can make borreltijd yours at home by making an event of it. I like to invite friends over early in the evening on a weekend—this is sometimes the best time to see friends, as I can catch them before they head off to their fun single-people evening activities. We fry up some cheese balls and bitterballen, put cashews in a bowl, and offer a wedge of cheese to slice from. Sometimes we fry up pieces of cod and some fries and serve with pickles and garlicky mayonnaise; other times we have a few Cheese Cookies (p. 92), olives, a bit of dried fruit, and a couple of gin and tonics. Borrels can be as simple or elaborate as you have the energy for, but the point is not to overdo it; borrels are meant to be gezellig (see p. 171) and gezellig is not strenuous or arduous. Ease into your borrels. Leisurely fry up some bitterballen. Slip into something comfortable. And proost!

Croquettes and Bitterballs

For the uninitiated, croquettes and bitterballs are fundamentally the same thing: finely chopped meat and veggies held together by a roux. The mixture is chilled, rolled into balls or logs, coated in flour, egg, and bread crumbs, and then deep-fried. The only thing that sets them apart is size and shape. Croquettes—kroketten—are generally eaten at meal times, either as large, single croquettes as the meat portion or on white bread with mustard, either open-faced or as a sandwich. Bitterballen—not actually bitter—are eaten as a borrel snack with a bitter beer or gin; you would order them with a beer in a restaurant or buy them pre-made from the freezer section of a supermarket to fry at home.

Making bitterballs or croquettes is a time-consuming process, one that in my household generally happens over a weekend in late December when we have a lot more free time. Because they are time-consuming, most Dutch people don't bother making these at home. A box of eighteen at the Albert Heijn supermarket in Amsterdam costs about €3; at a bar, you could order a dozen for the same price or less. When we visited Nick's family in Friesland, we visited a "patat," a kind of fry shop, and bought four big croquettes for dinner one night—we waited as they fried them for us, then wrapped them in brown paper, like take-away fish and chips. If they were that easy to come by, I wouldn't make them either.

However, in North America they are not widely available. Nick grew up in private Christian schools largely populated by Dutch families with kids who were first or second-generation Canadians, and recalls fondly the winter fairs at which grandmothers would sell their own homemade croquettes to raise funds for the school or for charity. His mother would occasionally pick them up at "the Dutch store," a market in New Westminster (near Vancouver in British Columbia) that sold Dutch groceries, and fry them up as a treat, mostly for Nick's dad or Frisian grandparents. As adults, we discovered them at a local Dutch restaurant, available frozen to be reheated at home at your convenience. All store-bought croquettes available in our area taste the same, leading me to believe there is a single croquette producer somewhere out there, if only we knew how to find them.

Because you can't just pop into the local supermarket and buy a bag of croquettes or bitterballs, most Dutch families in Canada have a family recipe that they make perhaps once a year. They are very much a treat, the kind of thing Nick and his friends look forward to (usually around the holidays). Some families have a tradition of getting together to make croquettes in large batches for the freezer, though Nick's immediate family is not one of them. I have made my disappointment known.

We used to make our own croquettes, but because it is a lot of work, I need to wrangle help, and for a long time the only person available to help was Nick. Unfortunately, Nick does not have the delicate, skilled hands of someone's Dutch grandmother, and every time he'd roll a croquette it would end up looking like a giant poop. I thought he'd get better at it, but he never did. Now we make bitterballs, which are a lot harder to mess up, even for Nick.

Most of the time we make bitterballs because, between us, we have three family Christmas dinners, and my parents, Nick's parents, and my aunt and uncle tend to send us home with a lot of leftovers, usually some combination of beef and turkey or ham. My parents in particular have a habit of making more food than even twice the number of Christmas dinner guests could possibly eat. (I like to make fun of them for this, but would never truly complain about it.) We use most of the leftover meat in bitterballs. The recipe that follows calls for uncooked meat, but just know that if you are facing ten Tupperware containers full of roast beef or turkey breast, you can easily cook that leftover meat in much the same way, skipping only the meat-browning stage right at the beginning.

If you are making turkey croquettes or bitterballs, replace the beer and herbs in the traditional recipe that follows in equal measure with white wine, fresh rosemary, and a bit of dried sage. And keep in mind that the recipe following makes just one batch—if you are going to all this trouble, double the recipe. After breading, line baking sheets with parchment paper and fill them up with bitterballs, then freeze them uncooked; once frozen, place in freezer bags and store for several months, frying as many as you need whenever you need them. I joke about my marriage a lot, but I am fairly certain a freezer full of bitterballs is legitimately the secret to mine.

The best way to make these is with the help of a food processor or meat grinder; if you don't have either of these, add an extra hour to cool the meat and veggies after simmering before chopping as finely as you can with a large knife.

Traditional Bitterballs

In bars and cafés in the Netherlands, these are often served with a grainy Dutch mustard akin to Dijon. At home, we serve them with yellow American mustard, Nick's preference.

6 tbsp butter, divided

1.5 lb (680 g) beef chuck, cubed

1 medium onion, chopped

1 carrot, chopped

1 celery stalk, chopped

3 garlic cloves, smashed

¾ cup (175 mL) lager or pilsner
   beer

1 bay leaf

1 sprig fresh thyme

1½ tsp kosher salt

2 tsp grainy Dijon mustard

1 tsp yellow curry powder

1¼ cup (310 mL) all-purpose
   flour, divided

½ tsp ground nutmeg

3 eggs, beaten

2 cups (500 mL) dry bread
   crumbs

4–6 cups neutral-tasting oil,
   such as canola, for frying

In a large pot on medium-high heat, melt 2 tbsp butter. Add cubed meat, and brown on all sides. Remove to a plate and set aside.

Add onions, carrot, celery, and garlic, and sauté until vegetables have just begun to sweat, about 4 minutes. Add beer, scraping bottom of pot to release browned bits, then return meat to pot. Add bay leaf and thyme sprig, then add 2 cups (500 mL) water. Reduce heat to medium.

Bring the pot to a simmer, then cook for 45 minutes. Strain liquid into a bowl, and remove thyme sprig and bay leaf. Mince meat using a food processor or meat grinder, or chop finely by hand. Set aside.

Return pot to stove. On medium heat, melt remainder of butter. Add salt, mustard, curry powder, and ¼ cup (60 mL) flour, and nutmeg, whisking to form a paste. Measure out 2 cups (500 mL) strained liquid and whisk into butter-flour mixture. Add more water if needed. Cook for 5–6 minutes, until thick and bubbling, whisking occasionally.

Return minced meat and vegetables to pot, and stir to thoroughly combine. Let cool to room temperature, then cover and refrigerate for at least 4 hours or up to 48.

Line a baking sheet with parchment paper.

Place remainder of flour in a pie plate. Place bowl of beaten eggs beside it, and a bowl of bread crumbs beside eggs. With clean hands, roll balls to 1½ in (4 cm) in diameter. Drop each ball in

Traditional Bitterballs cont'd

flour and roll to coat completely. Drop floured balls into beaten crumbs, and roll to coat completely. Roll crumbed balls between your palms to ensure coating sticks and is even; bitterballs that are not thoroughly coated will burst in oil when fried.

Line up balls on prepared baking sheet, and place in freezer for at least 30 minutes, or freeze completely to use another time.

In a large, heavy pot on high, heat oil to 375°F (190°C). Working in batches, fry up to 6 balls at a time until golden and crisp, 2–3 minutes. Drain on a plate lined with paper towels. Let oil come back to temperature between batches.

Serve bitterballs hot.

Paprika Bitterballs

In Aruba, we ate these chicken croquettes flavored with red bell peppers. They were especially good with cold rum and tonics, which we enjoyed on a patio in the summer sun—if you can swing it, this is a pleasant way to spend an afternoon. Cancel other plans if you have to.

6 tbsp butter, divided

1.5 lb (680 g) boneless, skinless chicken breast, cubed

1 medium onion, chopped

1 red bell pepper, chopped

1 celery stalk, chopped

3 garlic cloves, smashed

¾ cup (175 mL) dry white wine

1 bay leaf

1 sprig fresh thyme

1 ½ tsp kosher salt

2 tsp smoked paprika

1 tsp grainy Dijon mustard

½ tsp ground nutmeg

1¼ cup (310 mL) all-purpose flour, divided

3 eggs, beaten

2 cups (500 mL) dry bread crumbs

4–6 cups neutral-tasting oil, such as canola, for frying

In a large pot on medium-high heat, melt 2 tbsp butter. Add cubed meat, and brown on all sides. Remove to a plate and set aside.

Add onions, bell peppers, celery, and garlic cloves, and sauté until vegetables have just begun to sweat, about 4 minutes. Add wine, scraping bottom of pot to release browned bits, then return meat to pot.

Add bay leaf and thyme sprig, then add 2 cups (500 mL) water. Reduce heat to medium.

Simmer for 45 minutes. Strain liquid into a bowl, and remove thyme sprig and bay leaf. Mince meat using a food processor or meat grinder, or chop finely by hand. Set aside.

Return pot to stove. On medium heat, melt remainder of butter. Add salt, smoked paprika, mustard, nutmeg, and ¼ cup (60 mL) flour, whisking to form a paste. Measure out 2 cups (500 mL) strained liquid, and whisk into butter-flour mixture.

Top up with water as needed. Cook for 5–6 minutes, until thick and bubbling, whisking occasionally.

Return minced meat and vegetables to pot, and stir to thoroughly combine. Let cool to room temperature, then cover and refrigerate at least 4 hours or up to 48 hours.

Line a baking sheet with parchment paper.

Paprika Bitterballs cont'd

Place remainder of flour in a pie plate. Place bowl of beaten eggs beside it, and a bowl of bread crumbs beside eggs. With clean hands, roll balls to 1½ in (4 cm) in diameter.

Drop each ball in flour and roll to coat completely. Drop floured balls into beaten eggs, and roll to coat completely. Drop egg-covered balls in bread crumbs, and roll to coat completely. Roll crumbed balls between your palms to ensure coating sticks and is even; bitterballs that are not thoroughly coated will burst in oil when fried.

Line up balls on prepared baking sheet, and place in freezer for at least 30 minutes, or freeze completely to use another time.

In a large, heavy pot on high, heat oil to 375°F (190°C). Working in batches, fry up to 6 bitterballs at a time until golden and crisp, 2–3 minutes. Drain on a plate lined with paper towels. Let oil come back to temperature between batches.

Serve bitterballs hot.

Potato-Kale Bitterballs

These little balls are like stamppot fritters; they're a nice way to serve up something indulgent to your vegetarian guests. And they're "pretty much nutritious"—kale, but here for a good time.

½ lb (680 g) starchy potatoes, such as Russet

1 tbsp kosher salt

½ lb (225 g) kale, stalks removed

½ cup (225 g) butter

1 onion, finely chopped

4 garlic cloves, minced

1 tsp grainy Dijon mustard

4 oz (115 g) smoked Gouda, shredded

½ tsp nutmeg

2 egg yolks plus 3 beaten eggs, divided

1 cup (250 mL) all-purpose flour

2 cups (500 mL) dry bread crumbs

Peel and dice potatoes. Place in large pot with salt and cold water to cover. On high heat, bring to a boil and cook until tender, 15–20 minutes. Set aside. Meanwhile, rinse and pat kale dry. Finely chop. Set aside. In a frying pan on medium-high heat, melt butter. Add onions, and sauté until softened and translucent, 3–5 minutes. Add garlic, then kale. Cook until kale wilts but retains some of its bright color, about 6 minutes.

Pass cooked potatoes through a food mill into a large bowl. Stir in kale mixture. Taste, adjusting seasonings as needed. Let cool to room temperature, then cover and refrigerate for at least 4 hours or up to 48. Stir in mustard, shredded cheese, nutmeg and 2 egg yolks. Line a baking sheet with parchment paper.

Place flour in a pie plate. Place bowl of beaten eggs beside it, and a bowl of bread crumbs beside eggs. With clean hands, roll balls to about 1½ in (4 cm) in diameter. Drop each ball in flour and roll to coat completely. Drop floured balls into beaten eggs, and roll to coat completely. Drop egg-covered balls in bread crumbs, and roll to coat completely. Roll crumbed balls between your palms to ensure coating sticks and is even; bitterballs that are not thoroughly coated will burst in oil when fried. Line up balls on prepared baking sheet, and place in freezer for at least 30 minutes, or freeze completely to use another time.

In a large, heavy pot on high, heat oil to 375°F (190°C). Working in batches, fry up to 6 bitterballs at a time until golden and crisp, 2–3 minutes. Drain on a plate lined with paper towels. Let oil come back to temperature between batches.

Serve bitterballs hot.

Genever

"And since the public, as well as private, pretexts for *een borreltje* [a borrel] were so common and so frequent, it was very difficult for the church in its arraignments to apply the distinction between mere tipsiness and dead drunkenness with any consistency."
—Simon Schama, *The Embarrassment of Riches*

I have heard and read a lot about the value of traveling with children—and I'm sure it's great for them—but you never hear about the drawbacks, which are that children on vacation are children on sugar and not as much sleep, and they are very excited all the time. Travel is a test of their endurance, but it is also a test of yours. This is how I discovered genever (pronounced "yeh-nay-fer").

Genever (also spelled jenever) is known as Dutch gin but is sort of the precursor to gin, a botanical, juniper-dominant distilled malt spirit that once had primarily medicinal purposes and, in a way, still does. It's less "ginny" than gin, a little milder on the palate. There are young genevers, which are bright and refreshing in a tall glass with ice and tonic water with a squish of lime, and there are old genevers, aged in barrels until they are more like rye whiskeys with floral, spicy notes. I like both although I'm generally not a fan of gin.

Genever can be difficult to find outside of the Netherlands and Belgium, and the only variety I have been able to source close to home is the young, clear kind from Boomsma Distilleerderij. Ketel One, known in North America for its vodkas, originated as a genever distillery and in fact still produces the spirit, but it is hard to find in North America. Bols, also a Dutch distiller, produces genever as well; for added Dutchness, you can buy a bottle of Bols genever in a distinctive, reusable Delft Blue bottle—every Dutch-originated household seems to have an empty one kicking around on a bookshelf or mantle; Nick didn't know until recently that the bottle was actually for booze, it was so ubiquitous in the households of his childhood friends (his parents have one too).

We "discovered" genever partly by accident, as it was a cheap, clear liquor and we were on vacation. We stayed in a hotel in Aruba with a kitchenette and picked up a bottle of Ketel One genever to store in the freezer for after a long day of beach-hopping and pool-swimming with Hunter, who could have stayed in the water forever. It was always around 34°C (93°F) which, for our mild Canadian blood, was very hot, and so at the end of each day we melted onto the couch. The bottle of genever in the freezer got so cold that the liquid turned to syrup, and when mixed with tonic water was so refreshing I might have even stopped sweating for the duration of the drink.

In Rotterdam, we found a bottle of "oude" (old) genever at World of Drinks, a well-stocked liquor store at Markthal. Oude genever is made in the traditional style and aged—the one we bought had been aged for twelve years, so it was sweet and light caramel in color. Oude genever is ideal for sipping, either neat or with an ice cube, and flatters aged Gouda and cured sausage.

Typically, one would enjoy a drink or two of genever in the early evening, either at home or in a café or bar after work before dinner. Genever is best with borrels—a savory snack of cheese and sausage or maybe bitterballen, or a few marinated olives or some garlic shrimp. It is a pleasant way to ease into the end of the day, and very efficiently erases any residual office-related stresses you might have carried out of the workplace. It is a social drink, the kind of thing you might pour for friends on a Friday night before grabbing a late dinner somewhere. It's good.

It is also a tonic for the effects of traveling with young children—suddenly, the urgent need to try every bathroom in all of the Netherlands is not so irritating, and you find yourself agreeing to allow your little sugar monster to have yet another Nutella-slathered pannekoek for dinner. A sip or two of genever after a long day of train travel or exploring a city on foot will lift the tension from your neck and ease the pain in your feet; it will also make you feel very sophisticated and European, which is nice if you have spent the rest of your day feeling like a tacky tourist in brown hiking boots.

If you can't find genever, gin is a suitable replacement; some domestic distillers produce "Dutch-style" gin which is similar to genever but can't be marketed as such due to rules around the combination of ingredients that constitutes genever and domain-of-origin-type EU labeling requirements. Look for Amsterdam-style gin; in a pinch, London dry-style gin will do.

Garlic Shrimp

Cold shrimp in a garlic marinade are a refreshing foil for rich cheeses and fried meats; serve these with crisp crackers or on cucumber slices.

½ lb (250 g) peeled pink shrimp
1 garlic clove, minced
2 tbsp olive oil
1 tbsp white wine vinegar
½ tsp kosher salt
½ tsp ground black pepper
½ tsp crushed red pepper flakes
1 tbsp minced fresh basil

Pour shrimp into a colander and rinse thoroughly. Pat dry with paper towels.

In the bottom of a medium bowl, whisk together garlic, olive oil, wine vinegar, salt, pepper, red pepper flakes, and basil. Add shrimp and toss to coat. Spoon into a pint (500-mL) jar and seal. Refrigerate for at least 1 hour, or up to 24. Serve cold.

Herring

"[Herring] will make you apt to piss/ And you will not fail/
(With pardon) to shit/ And ceaselessly fart." —Jacob Westerbaen, 1656

Herring is everywhere in the Netherlands, and new herring is herring at its purest and most uncomplicated. New herring is young, caught in the late winter and early spring after it fattens up but before it's all gnarly and mature. It's served deboned and lightly brined, so that it still tastes freshly caught. The flesh is a bit firm—you can have it with pickles and minced raw onions if you like.

New herring is fisherman food and street food, and in the Netherlands you can find stalls and stands on roadsides and in town squares the way you might find hot dog vendors in North American cities. To eat new herring, you hold the fish up by its tail and bite from the bottom; it's a little slimy, with that oily fish flavor that some people need a bit of time to get used to, but worth the Euro-and-a-bit that it costs to try out. (If you find it too slippery and don't mind looking like a tourist, you can eat it with a knife and fork.) There's something about a bite of creamy, sort of oily fish on a cold spring day that feels very right, invigorating even—it's the sort of thing that just feels good to eat, like watermelon in summer or hot sauce on eggs after a night of drinking, because you can imagine it replacing something important, restoring something within you and making everything all right.

Although new herring is a seasonal treat, herring itself is a year-round food, and it's widely available canned, pickled, and cured. It appears frequently on restaurant menus in salads and on toast or rusks, and my favorite way to eat it is in crème fraîche or sour cream with cucumber, a bit of onion, and fresh dill on dark rye bread (p. 90). In many parts of North America, the herring season is very short, and fresh herring can be hard to come by; the fish are small and oily, so they go from fresh and briny to rancid and offensive as quickly as overnight. For that reason, herring is often available frozen or smoked whole, preserved in brine, or canned.

Herring, like mackerel and anchovies and sardines, are oily fish rich in brain-friendly docosahexaenoic acid (DHA) and vitamin D, which promotes calcium absorption—perhaps this is part of why so many in this dairy-loving nation are so tall? Herring make a cheap, nutritious snack and lend inexpensive protein to larger meals.

Historically, herring has been a patriotic dish and a source of pride for those—especially the Calvinists—who viewed more opulent dishes with lusty French sauces as immoral and dangerous; it's a simple fish for common people, not pretentious rich folk with no morals. There are poems and drinking songs about herring. It appears in etchings and still-life paintings. Herring matters a great deal to the Dutch.

Marinated Herring

You're most likely to find fresh local herring in spring, and if you're lucky enough to get a bunch, marinate it to serve with borrels, or to toss with potatoes for a delightful twist on potato salad (p. 216).

¼ cup (60 mL) + 1 tbsp kosher salt

1 lb (454 g) fresh herring, gutted

1 lemon

2 cups (500 mL) white wine vinegar

⅓ cup (80 mL) granulated sugar

1 bay leaf

1 tsp black peppercorns

½ tsp coriander seeds

2 shallots, thinly sliced

In a large pot on high, heat 3 cups (750 mL) water with ¼ cup salt until salt has dissolved completely. Let cool.

Cut herring into 1-in (2.5-cm) pieces, discarding heads and tails. Place herring pieces in a 9 x 13-in (3.5-L) baking pan, and pour cooled salt water over top. Cover tightly, and refrigerate for 24 hours.

Scrub lemon under hot running water, and dry with a clean kitchen towel. Using a vegetable peeler, peel just the yellow part of the rind off in large strips. Juice lemon after it's been peeled. Set aside.

Bring vinegar, sugar, lemon juice, bay leaf, peppercorns, coriander seeds, and remaining salt to a boil, stirring until sugar has completely dissolved. Set aside to cool completely.

Rinse a 1-qt (1-L) jar or 2 pint (500-mL) jars under hot water, and dry with a clean kitchen towel. Place lemon peel in jar. Alternate layers of herring and thinly sliced shallots, then pour cooled vinegar mixture over top. Cover jar with a tight-fitting lid. Refrigerate for 3 days before serving; store in refrigerator for up to 2 weeks.

Creamed Herring

Serve creamed herring on Dutch rusks or rye crispbreads with sliced boiled eggs and dill pickles for a pleasant weekend lunch (herring and boiled eggs are not a good desk lunch if you work in an office and like to have good relationships with your co-workers). Store-bought or homemade marinated herring (p. 89) will work equally well.

½ lb (250 g) marinated herring
½ cup (125 mL) sour cream or
    hangop (p. 246)
4 green onions, finely chopped
¼ cup (60 mL) fresh dill, finely
    chopped
1 tbsp white wine vinegar
1 tsp kosher salt
½ tsp ground black pepper

Coarsely chop marinated herring and place in a bowl. Using a fork, mix in sour cream, green onions, dill, vinegar, salt, and pepper. Serve immediately.

Curry Cashews

MAKES 1 CUP (250 ML)

I wanted to specify serving size for this recipe, but to be honest, I have never really successfully measured how many people these will feed—because they mostly feed me. Make a double batch if you think you'd like to share with friends. Even then, I bet you still won't.

1 cup (250 g) raw, unsalted cashews

1 tbsp melted butter

2 tsp Maggi

1 tsp yellow curry powder

½ tsp crushed red pepper flakes

Preheat oven to 350°F (175°C).

Spread cashews in a single layer on a rimmed baking sheet. Drizzle with melted butter, and use your hands to make sure each nut has been sufficiently buttered.

Roast for 5 minutes. Remove pan from oven, gently shake to flip nuts, then return to oven. Roast for 5–6 more minutes, checking periodically to ensure they don't burn, until sizzling and golden.

Pour cashews into a large bowl. Sprinkle in Maggi and spices, and toss to coat. Allow to cool, then serve. Store in a tightly sealed container for up to 3 days.

BORRELS (DUTCH TAPAS) |91

Cheese Cookies

These little balls are addictive—they're like a classier version of Cheetos, all savory and moreish. Nick and I barely manage to transfer these off the baking sheet into a bowl. They are meant to go with gin, but they are also very tasty with a big frosty pint of bitter beer—try both ways and decide for yourself what you prefer.

1 cup (250 mL) room-
temperature butter

½ cup (125 mL) finely grated
aged cheese, such as Gouda
or Parmesan

1 tsp kosher salt

1 tsp ground black pepper

½ cup (125 mL) whole milk

2 tbsp gin

2 cups all-purpose flour

2 tsp baking powder

Preheat oven to 350°F (175°C).

In a large bowl, cream together butter, cheese, salt, and pepper. Add milk and gin, continuing to mix until well combined. Scrape down sides of bowl.

In a separate bowl, whisk together flour and baking powder.

Mix wet ingredients and dry ingredients to form a dough.

Line a baking sheet with parchment.

Form dough balls about ½ in (1 cm) in diameter, and place 1 in (2.5 cm) apart on prepared baking sheet (in a couple of batches).

Bake for 15 minutes, until just golden and lightly puffed. Serve warm.

Fried Cheese Balls

These are kind of like if you crossed a cheese souffle with a doughnut, and they are pretty fantastic. We first tried these at a barbecue restaurant in the Caribbean, and then found something strikingly similar pre-made and sold in packages in a cheese shop in Haarlem. They are at their best when you eat them in a backyard in summer.

4 cups (1 L) canola or other neutral oil

8 oz (225 g) medium Cheddar cheese

3 eggs

1 tbsp sambal oelek

½ cup (125 mL) all-purpose flour

1 tsp baking soda

1 tsp kosher salt

In a large, heavy pot such as a Dutch oven, heat oil on high to about 375°F (190°C).

Grate cheese into a large bowl. Stir in eggs, sambal oelek, flour, baking soda, and salt, and combine well to form a pasty dough. Divide into 4 equal portions, and then divide each portion into 4 equal portions. Roll each portion firmly into a ball.

Working in batches, drop balls into hot oil, and fry for about 3 minutes, until golden. Drain on a plate lined with paper towels, and serve hot.

Cheese Cigars

One thing I appreciate about the Dutch is that despite the excellent quality of their cheese, they are not content to always simply eat it as it is; they have a whole host of ways to bake it, melt it, and fry it. This version of fried cheese was one we enjoyed one lazy afternoon in Rotterdam, pausing for an hour in a café for a beer before the train ride back to where we were staying. This recipe makes 12, but it's the easiest thing in the world, and you can multiply by as much as you need to.

6 oz (170 g) mild cheese, such as medium Cheddar or brick Gouda

12 store-bought wonton wrappers

2–4 cups (500 mL–1 L) canola or other neutral oil

Fill a small bowl with cold water.

Trim cheese into sticks about 3 in (7.5 cm) long.

Working on a flat surface, lay out 1 wonton wrapper in the shape of a diamond. Dip your index finger into water, and drag it along top two sides of wrapper.

Place a cheese stick on lower third of wrapper, then fold bottom point over cheese. Roll wrapper upward over cheese, folding corners over ends, to top third of wrapper. Press down onto the cheese to seal like an envelope. Repeat with remaining cheese sticks.

In a large, heavy pot such as a Dutch oven, heat oil on high to 375°F (190°C).

Working in batches, fry cigars for about 90 seconds, until golden and crisp. Drain on a plate lined with paper towels, and serve hot.

Kibbeling

Kibbeling is cod or other firm white fish cut into bite-sized pieces and fried. In the Netherlands, they are served in a little tray with two sections, with a slightly sweet tartar sauce in the smaller side. When I make this for borrels with Hunter, he takes his with a couple of slices of watermelon and a glass of chocolate milk; you may prefer to sub the milk for cold beer.

1 lb (454 g) cod
1 cup (250 mL) pilsner or lager
   beer
4 egg yolks
3 tsp kosher salt, divided
1 tsp grainy Dijon mustard
2–4 cups (500 mL–1 L) canola
   or other neutral oil
1½ cups (350 mL) all-purpose
   flour
1 tsp yellow curry powder

Trim cod into bite-sized pieces. (They can be irregular in size.)

In a large bowl, whisk together beer, egg yolks, 2 tsp salt, and mustard. Add cod chunks to beer mixture, and let marinate for 30 minutes.

In a large, heavy pot such as a Dutch oven, heat oil on high to 375°F (190°C).

In a large bowl, combine flour, curry powder, and remainder of salt, and mix well. Dredge fish in flour mixture to coat thoroughly.

Working in 2 batches, fry fish pieces for 3–6 minutes, until golden. (I err on the longer side, because fish steams as it cooks and can soften the crust if removed too early.) Drain fish on a plate lined with paper towels. Let oil come back to temperature between batches.

Serve hot.

Dutch Fries

I have made fries in all kinds of ways, and while I was working on this book I waffled between two ways. The "official" way, which is to double-fry the potatoes, produces very delicious, deeply golden fries, but is kind of a hassle, especially if, like me, you're a messy, occasionally chaotic cook. The other way I learned about by binge-watching *America's Test Kitchen*: Cook the fries as if you were simply boiling them, but instead of water, use oil. I brine and then dry mine before cooking for a more complex flavor. Serve with Garlic Mayonnaise (p. 247) or Curry Ketchup (p. 251), or use as the base for Hairdresser Fries (opposite).

½ cup (125 mL) + 2 tsp kosher salt, divided

2.2 lb (1 kg) yellow-fleshed potatoes, such as Yukon gold, peeled and cut into sticks about ½-in (1-cm) thick

4–6 cups (1–1.5 L) canola or other neutral oil

Fill a large bowl with 6 cups (1.5 L) room temperature water, and whisk in ½ cup (125 mL) kosher salt until salt dissolves. Place potato sticks in brine and let sit for 5 minutes.

Remove potatoes. Place on a baking sheet lined with clean dish towels or paper towels, and let air-dry for about 10 minutes. Pat dry thoroughly to absorb all moisture.

Place dried potatoes in large, heavy-bottomed pot such as a Dutch oven, so that tops form an even layer. Add oil to cover.

On high heat, bring oil to a boil, uncovered, then cook, stirring very gently and occasionally to prevent sticking and scorching for 10–15 minutes, until potatoes are soft but not yet browned.

Meanwhile, dry baking sheet, and layer with fresh paper towels. Stir potatoes gently. Boil for an additional 4–6 minutes, until golden and crisp.

Using a slotted spoon or a fish spatula, remove fries from oil to baking sheet to drain. Sprinkle with 2 tsp salt, and serve hot.

Let oil cool, then strain into a jar and reserve for another use.

Hairdresser Fries

I thought "hairdresser fries" was just a weird accident of Google Translate and kind of loved it, but it turns out that's the actual name for this dish—kipsalon—and though it is a relatively recent addition to Dutch cuisine, it is spectacular in its multilayered multi-culturalness (just like the Netherlands). It's pretty much a heap of fries topped with shawarma meat, cheese, and fresh veggies—somewhere between Dutch poutine and Turkish nachos—and it's downright debaucherous. I have to stop making it for family dinner, because this is straight-up booze food. Tater Tots are not traditional, but I'm a monster and would *definitely* talk you into kipsalon tots late one night. Serve with Garlic Mayonnaise (p. 247) and your favorite hot sauce.

1 batch Dutch Fries (p. 98), or equal weight store-bought frozen French fries or Tater Tots, prepared according to package instructions

3 tbsp olive oil

4 garlic cloves, minced

1 lb (454 g) boneless, skinless chicken thighs, diced

2 tsp kosher salt

2 tsp smoked paprika

1 tsp ground cumin

½ tsp ground coriander

½ tsp ground black pepper

¼ tsp ground cinnamon

1 lemon, zest and juice

4 oz (115 g) shredded Cheddar or Edam cheese

½ lb (250 g) fresh tomatoes, diced

½ head Bibb or Butter lettuce, roughly torn

4 green onions, minced

Preheat oven to broil.

Place prepared fries or tots in a 9 x 13-in (3.5-L) baking dish.

In a frying pan on medium-high, heat olive oil until shimmering. Add garlic, diced chicken thighs, salt, paprika, cumin, coriander, pepper, and cinnamon, and sauté for about 6 minutes, until chicken is cooked through, spices have darkened, and pan looks dry. Add lemon zest and squeeze lemon juice over top, tossing to coat. Remove skillet from heat.

Spoon half of mixture over fries. Scatter half of cheese over top, then add remainder of chicken and cheese.

Broil for 4–6 minutes, until bubbling and golden (check every minute after 3 minutes). Remove from oven.

Top with diced tomatoes, lettuce, and green onions. Serve hot.

Uitsmijter

Uitsmijter (pronounced "out-smiter") is somewhere between a midnight snack and breakfast, traditionally the kind of thing you'd eat after getting thrown out of a bar for rowdiness or after stumbling home from a party. The word uitsmijter means "bouncer," or the person who would toss you out of a place after you had behaved poorly (not that I would know anything about that because I am a lady, and I can't hear you scoff from here so it stands). You can serve this as a handheld sandwich or open-faced, depending on whether you plan to cook up one or two eggs. Serve with a large glass of water and some pickles straight from the jar.

1 tbsp canola or other neutral oil

1–2 eggs

2 tsp room-temperature butter

2 thick slices soft white or dark rye bread

1 tsp grainy Dijon mustard

1 oz (25 g) thinly sliced Gouda cheese

2 oz (50 g) thinly sliced deli ham

1 small tomato, thinly sliced

salt and pepper, to taste

Preheat oven to 350°F (175°C).

In a frying pan on high, heat oil. Crack egg(s) into pan. Once whites begin to turn opaque, about 30 seconds, put pan into oven and turn off heat. Set a timer for 5 minutes.

Meanwhile, butter both slices of bread, and spread mustard on 1 slice. Pile cheese, ham, and tomato slices on bread. Sprinkle tomatoes with pinch of black pepper.

Place cooked egg on tomato slices, then sprinkle with a pinch of salt and another pinch of pepper, if desired.

Top with second slice of bread, then eat the whole thing standing over the kitchen sink before heading straight to bed.

WEEKNIGHT DINNERS

WEEKNIGHT DINNERS

As I write this, the last bit of December snow is melting into slush puddles on the sidewalk outside while Hunter naps in his fleece pajamas on our ratty old couch beside the fireplace. The cat found the warm pile of laundry I didn't get to folding this morning and has kept it warm since lunchtime. On the stove, meatballs are braising, and a pot of tea is not quite steeped. It's been dark in the afternoons for a few weeks now and the slightest effort feels extravagant. It is after Christmas, so we have spent all of our dollars, but there is nothing left to buy. Now is the time for frugality, for tidying up, for staying at home, and for simple dishes that are mostly nutritious but also involve enough cheese to be a balm over January's austerities. I hate this weather, and I'm sad about my bank account, but I love this time of year.

By this time every year, I've had more than my fair share of complicated meals, of elaborate feasts full of many dishes, and sitting upright for too long. Now is the time for one-pot dinners, for mains big enough to stretch into lunches the next day, for food that nurtures as much as it nourishes. I want crisp salads, veggie-filled casseroles, big fat meatballs, and meals I can pull out of thin air, just "whatever's in the crisper" and some condiments if possible. I don't have time, especially on weeknights.

This feeling of having no time, of being stretched very thin, is not particularly Dutch. Dutch mothers are famously patient, and equality between the sexes is an important aspect of Dutch culture. Fewer than ten percent of Dutch women work full time; the majority work part time and seem to prefer it. In a 2009 column on VoxEU.org, the policy portal for the Center for Economic Policy Research, researchers describe a failure of the Dutch government to mobilize women to work more than part-time through tax incentives; according to the authors, "only four percent of women working part-time would prefer to work full time." According to the same piece, "about forty percent of both Dutch men and women think that the family would suffer if the woman would work full time." This opinion has not changed much during the past decades and across generations. Although part-time work among men is higher in the Netherlands than in most other countries, men are not expected to reduce their working hours when there are young children in the family. And while women—single and married women with children—tend to prefer to work part-time, they use their time well—they care for children, but they also pursue their interests, socialize in the afternoons, and make the most of their free time.

On the one hand, I find this jarring—I have a demanding career in an expensive city, and can't imagine not working full time, partly to support my family but partly because my identity is—in a very North American way—tied up in "what I do." (Is this healthy? Probably not. And my feet always hurt and I believe I am personally sustaining the Vancouver pantyhose market.) If there was a way to work fewer hours in a satisfying job while retaining financial independence—that would truly be having it all. I'd lean into that!

A lot of Dutch food is comfort food, and nowhere is that more apparent than at the Dutch dinner table. At my dinner table, it is no different, with my own tall, stubborn child partial to soothing, straightforward dishes. If I don't have it in me to fight about dinner, we'll have one of the recipes that follow, likely the Dutch meatballs (on rice if I'm being kind to him, on hutspot if all he's eaten that week was sandwiches—I am as harried a working mom as there ever was), or the chicken curry that is more like the curries of my suburban Canadian childhood than anything you might find in a place where there are whole markets for spices. These are not challenging meals to make or consume, and they will warm your home when you need them to.

Some of the dishes in this chapter are traditionally Dutch, and some were brought home by the Dutch from their travels and adapted to the ingredients and tastes at home. Dutch Macaroni (p. 125) is a staple food, a bit like American goulash; it's impossible to not make too much

of it, which means enough leftovers for lunch the next day. Nasi Goreng (p. 148), made vegetarian here, is a little Indonesian and so ubiquitous that each Dutch family has its own recipe (or preferred store-bought mix). Keeshi Yena (p. 112) is a Creole Aruban dish, a satisfying stew of chicken, vegetables, nuts, and dried fruit stuffed between generous layers of melted Gouda. Pom (p. 117) is the national dish of Suriname, a casserole of chicken and taro with allspice and citrus juices, but in the Netherlands it's been adapted to include potatoes instead of taro.

Typically the Dutch eat one hot, substantial meal per day (though this is not a hard-and-fast rule, by any means). If the hot meal happens midday, then the evening meal will often be a cold dish, primarily involving bread. This chapter assumes you'd have your hot meal somewhere around 6:00 p.m., though a plate of cold meat and hearty bread is always sufficient for dinner, at least as far as I'm concerned.

And if you are very tired and the dark months have begun to feel long and you are overworked and summer seems impossibly far away, many of these dishes are well-suited to dinner on the couch; dishes like the braised endive with bacon, topped with poached egg (p. 126) will suit one or two people and pair very nicely with beer and stretch pants and the latest Idris Elba experience.

We do what we have to do to get through so many long days, whether that's comfort food or stir-fried leftovers or breaking with the routine, even just this once.

Pancakes

You can get all kinds of pancakes in the Netherlands, from drie in de pan—which means "three in the pan" and is most like what we'd serve for breakfast in North America—and "American-style" pancakes, which are larger, like diner pancakes, fluffy with buttermilk and covered in schenkstroop, a pancake-specific golden syrup that's not as dark or thick as regular stroop. But the best pancakes—and Hunter's all-time favorite—are pannekoek.

Pannekoek are thin, plate-sized pancakes, usually 12 in (30 cm) in diameter; they're thicker and heartier than a crêpe and have traditionally been made with a combination of white and buckwheat flours. Here, I've provided a recipe for pannekoek with rye flour (p. 107). Pannenkoeken are lightly yeasted and generally served at dinner. At a pannekoekhuis, you can order sweet or savory versions; Hunter's favorite is always a pannekoek with Nutella, but I like mine with oude kaas (aged cheese) and tomatoes. Many of the savory (and some of the fruit-based sweet) pancakes are made by cooking the toppings into the pancake; they are best when the cheese gets crispy in parts but stays melted in others.

Pancakes have been part of European cuisines since at least the fifteenth century, but recipes did not begin to appear until later. A book written for wealthy Dutch households in the seventeenth century details several approaches to pancake cookery; personally, I am quite fond of the instructions "to fry common pancakes" (different from the notes on how "to fry the best kind of pancakes"). Excerpted and translated by Peter G. Rose in *The Sensible Cook: Dutch Foodways in the Old and New World* (1989), "common pancakes" from 1667 are not fundamentally different from a modern pancake recipe: "For each pond of wheat-flour, take a pint of sweet milk and three eggs. Some add some sugar to it." (A pond was a variable measurement that equaled about a pound, with a few ounces difference depending on region; after the metric system was introduced in 1816, a pond became equal to a kilogram, or about 2.2 pounds.)

When we make pannenkoeken at home, it's a lazy meal—I fry up maybe four pancakes, then pop as many as Nick and I would like into the oven with a bit of whatever cheese we have on hand to melt. I put Hunter's on a big plate, and offer Nutella, jam, hagelslaag, and maple syrup. For Nick and me, I fry an egg or two, and serve sautéed mushrooms, fresh spinach, or cold sliced tomatoes and deli ham. In spring, some blanched asparagus and soft scrambled egg make a light but satisfying filling. When we've got not-quite-enough leftover Nasi Goreng (p. 148) or Babi Ketjap (p. 164), it can be nice to stretch a little bit into a meal by stuffing the leftovers into a pannekoek—provide a few condiments and fresh toppings to make the meal seem new and different.

Basic Rye Pannenkoek

(MAKES 4 SERVINGS)

We mostly make these for dinner, but they also make a very hearty weekend breakfast for guests. If you plan to feed more than a few people, you can double the batch and make these a few minutes ahead; layer them on a baking sheet and keep between layers of parchment in an oven set to low heat (200°F [94°C]) as you cook enough for everyone. Serve with a variety of sweet and savory toppings for each person to customize her own.

2 cups (500 mL) lukewarm
    whole milk
1 tbsp granulated sugar
¼ tsp dry yeast
2 eggs, beaten
2 tbsp melted butter
½ cup (125mL) all-purpose
    flour
½ cup (125mL) dark rye flour

In a large bowl, whisk together milk, sugar, and yeast, and let stand for 5 minutes, until yeast has begun to froth and appears fluffy. Whisk in eggs, melted butter, and both flours and let stand at room temperature for at least 30 and up to 60 minutes.

Working in batches, ladle about ½ cup (125 mL) batter into a lightly greased or non-stick 12-in (30-cm) frying pan on medium heat. Working quickly, gently spread batter around pan with bottom of ladle.

Cook for 1–2 minutes, until bubbles appear on top of pancake. Using a fork or slotted spatula, flip and cook for an additional minute, until pancake slides easily out of pan onto a plate.

Sautéed Mushrooms for Pannenkoek

Serve a couple of spoonfuls of sautéed mushrooms on a weeknight pannenkoek with sliced or grated Gouda and mustard.

¼ cup (60 mL) butter

2 garlic cloves, minced

1 tsp minced fresh thyme

1 lb (454 g) white button or cremini mushrooms, sliced

½ tsp kosher salt

¼ tsp ground black pepper

¼ tsp ground nutmeg

⅓ cup (80 mL) dry white wine

In a frying pan on medium-high heat, melt butter. Add garlic and thyme, and cook for 1 minute. Add mushrooms, spreading evenly across surface of pan, and cook for about 2 minutes, until liquid has sweated out of mushrooms. Sprinkle with salt.

Stirring occasionally, cook until liquid has reduced, about 3 more minutes. Add pepper and nutmeg, then deglaze pan with wine. Cook until liquid has reduced again, another 3 minutes. Serve inside or on top of Rye Pannenkoeken (p. 107).

VanderWoud Cheese Toasties

· MAKES 4–6 PIECES ·

Everyone has a weird thing they eat at home, away from the judgmental eyes of normal people, and the VanderWoud kids are no different. They'd split a couple of soft white dinner rolls, slice Gouda from the huge wedge always in the refrigerator, cut a couple of pieces of raw bacon into bun-length strips, and microwave these to just melt the cheese and—hopefully—cook the bacon. This is an updated, food-safe version of that. Will serve 4 normals or one VanderWoud.

2 strips bacon

½ cup (125 mL) room-
temperature butter

4 oz (115 g) finely shredded
medium Gouda

1 tsp grainy Dijon mustard

½ tsp ground black pepper

4–6 thick slices of soft white
bread

Preheat oven to broil.

In a frying pan on medium-high heat, fry bacon slices for 2–3 minutes per side until crisp. Finely chop cooked bacon.

In a small bowl, mash together bacon, butter, Gouda, mustard, and pepper.

Lay slices of bread on a baking sheet, and broil 3–5 minutes, until golden.

Remove bread from oven, flip, and spread cheese mixture over top. Broil for 5–7 minutes, until edges appear crisp and cheese is melty, bubbly, and golden. Rotate pan once during broiling to ensure even browning.

Serve hot, dishing these out on individual plates if your Vander-Woud can be seen lurking nearby with intent to steal.

Tomato-Paprika Soup

This is pure comfort food, the kind of thing you can make in winter with a couple of hot-house bell peppers—which are "paprika" in Dutch—to hint at summer. Roasting the peppers brings out their sweetness and makes it easy to remove the skins. Serve with a tosti—a grilled ham and cheese sandwich.

1 lb (454 g) red bell peppers

3 tbsp olive oil, divided

1 onion, trimmed and diced

1 celery stalk, trimmed and diced

1 carrot, trimmed, peeled, and diced

2 garlic cloves, chopped

2 tsp kosher salt

1 tsp ground black pepper

1 tsp smoked paprika

½ tsp ground cumin

28-oz (196-mL) can whole tomatoes

4 cups (1 L) homemade or low-sodium chicken stock

2 sprigs fresh thyme

1 bay leaf

½ cup (125 mL) heavy cream

Preheat oven to 400°F (200°C).

Rub peppers all over with 1 tbsp olive oil and set on a baking sheet lined with parchment paper. Roast, turning once at 30 minutes, for 60 minutes. Remove roasted peppers to a glass bowl, cover with plastic wrap, and let stand for 10 minutes.

In a heavy-bottomed pot on medium-high, heat remainder of oil. Add onions, celery, carrots, garlic, and salt, and sauté for about 4 minutes, until vegetables have brightened in color. Add pepper, paprika, and cumin, and stir to coat; sauté for an additional 2 minutes.

Peel skins off red peppers. Run a paring knife along inner membrane to remove seeds. Discard skins, seeds, and stem, then add peppers to pot.

Add tomatoes and chicken stock. Using kitchen string, tie thyme sprigs and bay leaf together, and submerge in cooking liquid. Bring to a boil, then reduce heat to medium. Simmer for 15 minutes, until vegetables are tender.

Using an immersion or stand blender, purée soup until smooth. Use care when working with hot liquids, and if using a stand blender, work in batches; do not fill more than halfway, as hot liquids expand and, well, kind of explode.

Return soup to pot on medium heat and bring to a simmer. Taste, adjusting seasonings as needed. Whisk in cream, and serve immediately.

Mussel Soup with Saffron

This is a dish that seems luxurious, but I only make it when mussels are on sale and I already have wine in the fridge. It's quick enough to pull together on a weeknight—I serve it as dinner with thick slices of toasted pumpernickel slathered in salted butter. With a quick greens and herbs salad (p. 213) and a glass of sparkling wine, this is also a fabulous weekend lunch for company.

3 lb (1.4 kg) mussels

4 cups (1 L) low-sodium or homemade chicken stock

pinch saffron or saffron extract (p. 19)

2 tbsp butter

1 shallot, minced

2 garlic cloves, minced

1 lb (500 g) starchy potatoes (such as Russet), diced

2 tsp kosher salt

½ tsp red pepper flakes

½ tsp ground black pepper

1 cup (250 mL) dry white wine

½ cup (125 mL) heavy cream

salt and pepper, to taste

½ cup (125 mL) roughly chopped fresh parsley

Look over mussels, discarding any that are broken or won't close when squeezed. Wash mussels and, using a clean pair of tweezers, remove beards—the hairy bits poking out from the side of the shell.

In a saucepan on medium-high heat, bring chicken stock and saffron to a simmer. Reduce heat to low.

Meanwhile, in a heavy pot on medium-high heat, melt butter. Add shallots, garlic, and potatoes, and stir to coat in butter. Add salt, pepper flakes, and pepper, then add mussels. Cover with a lid and cook for 5 minutes.

Remove lid, and carefully transfer mussels from pot to a large bowl. Discard any mussels that didn't open.

Add wine and warmed chicken stock to pot, and bring to a simmer. Cook for about 15 minutes, until potatoes are tender.

Meanwhile, carefully remove mussels from shells. Divide shelled mussels between four soup bowls, and set aside.

When potatoes are soft, stir in cream. Taste, adjusting seasonings as needed. Pour potatoes and broth into prepared bowls, then sprinkle with parsley to serve.

Keeshi Yena

········ MAKES 4 SERVINGS ········

I first tasted this dish in Aruba at The Old Cunucu House restaurant. It's a dish that was originally prepared by Indigenous slaves using discarded cheese-wheel scraps; traditionally, it might include raisins, olives, capers, nuts, or hot peppers, among other things, in a range of combinations and to suit the cook's taste. While I serve this at home in a 1.5-quart/1.4-liter round baking dish, you could portion it in four individual ramekins and freeze for reheating later. Serve with a light green salad and good white bread for sopping up the sauce.

2 tsp kosher salt, divided

1 lb (454 g) boneless, skinless chicken breasts or thighs

2 tbsp olive oil, divided

1 onion, diced

1 red bell pepper, diced

2 celery stalks, diced

4 garlic cloves, minced

2 tsp smoked paprika

1 tsp ground black pepper

½ tsp ground cumin

¼ tsp cayenne pepper

½ cup (125 mL) dry white wine

14-oz (398-mL) can crushed tomatoes

1 tbsp capers, roughly chopped

2 tsp Worcestershire sauce

3 oz (75 g) dried pitted prunes, roughly chopped

1 lime, juiced

salt and pepper, to taste

7 oz (200 g) sliced Gouda

½ cup (125 mL) roasted cashews

Sprinkle salt on both sides of chicken.

In a large frying pan on medium-high, heat 1 tbsp olive oil. Brown chicken, cooking about 10 minutes per side. Remove from heat and set chicken aside.

Add remainder of olive oil to pan, then add onions, bell peppers, celery, garlic and remainder of salt. Sauté for 2–3 minutes, until vegetables have brightened in color. Stir in smoked paprika, pepper, cumin, and cayenne pepper, and coat vegetables with spices.

Deglaze pan with wine, scraping any browned bits off bottom, and reduce heat to medium. Add crushed tomatoes, capers, Worcestershire sauce, and prunes. Cube cooled chicken and add to pan with lime juice. Simmer for about 10 minutes, until sauce has reduced and thickened slightly.

Taste and adjust seasonings. Set aside, and cool to room temperature. (You can do this up to 3 days ahead—it's better when made at least 1 day in advance; just cool and refrigerate until you're ready to assemble the casserole.)

Preheat oven to 350°F (175°C).

Line a lightly greased 1.5-qt (1.4-L) baking dish with slices of Gouda. They need not overlap by much, but should all be touch-

CONTINUED ON P.114

Pom

This citrusy chicken casserole is a very bright dish to offset a very gray day. Pom is the national dish of Suriname, though it was adapted in the Netherlands to use ingredients available there (i.e., potatoes); the result is a veggie-filled dish with lemon, lime, and orange, and gentle spice notes from the curry powder and allspice. Serve with a Lettuce Salad with Herbs (p. 213).

4 lb (1.8 kg) yellow-fleshed potatoes, such as Yukon Gold
6 tbsp butter, divided
1 onion, diced
2 carrots, peeled and diced
2 celery stalks, peeled and diced
1 red bell pepper, diced
3 garlic cloves, minced
2 Roma tomatoes, diced
1 lb (454 g) ground chicken
2 tsp kosher salt, divided
2 tsp yellow curry powder
1 tsp ground turmeric, divided
½ tsp ground allspice
3 tbsp all-purpose flour
½ cup (125 mL) orange juice
2 cups (500 mL) low-sodium or homemade chicken stock
1 lime, zest and juice
1 lemon, zest and juice
salt and pepper, to taste
1 egg, beaten

Preheat oven to 375°F (190°C).

Peel and dice potatoes. In a large pot of water on high heat, bring potatoes to a boil and cook for 15–20 minutes, until tender. Drain and set aside.

Meanwhile, melt 2 tbsp butter in a frying pan on medium-high heat. Add diced onions, carrots, celery, bell peppers, garlic, and tomatoes, and sauté for about 6 minutes, until vegetables have begun to sweat. Crumble ground chicken into pan, stirring to mix. Sauté for about 5 minutes, until chicken is mostly cooked.

Add 1 tsp salt, curry powder, ½ tsp turmeric, allspice, and flour, and stir to coat. Stir in orange juice, and cook for about 2 minutes, until liquid dissipates. Add chicken stock and lime zest and juice, and simmer for about 3 minutes, until thickened. Taste, adjusting seasonings as needed.

Meanwhile, mix remainder of butter, salt, and turmeric into cooked and drained potatoes with lemon zest and juice and beaten egg.

Transfer chicken mixture into a 9 x 13-in (3.5-L) baking dish. Spoon potato mixture over top, smoothing to cover chicken mixture. Drag a fork over potato topping to score surface.

Bake for 25 minutes, until topping is golden and filling is bubbly.

Let rest for 15 minutes before serving.

Herring Fritters with Onion Sauce

Herring and onions are a quintessentially Dutch combination, and very wallet-friendly. As weeknight dishes go, this one's fairly easy to pull together; if you don't have herring, a can of mackerel or salmon—or any leftover fish from last night's dinner—will work just fine. Serve with Cucumber Salad (p. 131) or steamed green beans. Nick likes his with hot sauce, and Hunter assures me this is delicious with ketchup.

2 cups (500 mL) cooked long-grain white rice

7 oz (200g) canned or smoked herring

1 celery stalk, minced

4 green onions, minced

2 eggs

½ cup (125 mL) bread crumbs

1 lemon, zest and juice

1 tsp grainy Dijon mustard

3 tsp kosher salt, divided

1 tsp yellow curry powder

½ tsp ground black pepper

2 tbsp butter

½ lb (454 g) onions, diced

1 cup (250 mL) whole milk

canola or other neutral oil, for frying

In a large bowl, combine rice, herring, celery, green onions, eggs, bread crumbs, lemon zest and juice, mustard, 2 tsp salt, curry powder, and pepper. Using your hands, mix thoroughly. Let stand 15 minutes.

Meanwhile, in a saucepan on medium heat, melt butter. Add onions, and sauté until softened and liquid has disappeared. Do not allow them to brown. Add 1 tsp salt, pour in milk, and cook for about 5 minutes, just until milk comes to a boil.

Remove onion mixture from heat and purée using an immersion blender or, working in batches, in a stand blender. Use care when blending hot liquids, and if using a stand blender, fill only halfway. Return to pan and keep warm on low heat, stirring occasionally, while cooking fritters.

In a frying pan on medium-high, heat 1 in (2.5 cm) oil until shimmering. Form herring mixture into 10 "cakes" with hands, and place gently into hot oil. Cook about 2 minutes per side, until crisp and golden.

To serve, pour onion sauce onto a plate and top with herring fritters.

Poached Salmon & Buttered Leeks

MAKES 4 SERVINGS

This is a very mild, light dish for an evening in spring or early summer when you just need something simple. Serve with a blob of mustard and buttered bread and, since it is calorically pretty light, a couple of cold gin and sodas to make up the difference. This dish pairs nicely with Sugar Snap Peas With Herb Vinaigrette (p. 130).

4 pieces skinless salmon fillet, about 5 oz (140 g) each

3 lemons, 2 thinly sliced, 1 quartered

3 tbsp gin

1 tbsp + 1 tsp kosher salt, divided

1 tsp ground black pepper

1 sprig fresh dill

1 bay leaf

3 tbsp butter

1 lb (454 g) leeks, white and light-green parts only, trimmed, rinsed, and finely chopped

Trim salmon pieces to an even thickness; save scraps for another use.

Layer slices from 2 lemons in a large pot or deep frying pan. Place salmon pieces on top of lemons. Drizzle with gin, then sprinkle with 1 tbsp salt and the pepper. Nestle dill and bay leaf in among salmon pieces. Cover salmon with ½ in (1.25 cm) cold water.

With pot on medium, heat water to about 170°F (75°C), and cook salmon until it reaches an internal temperature of 120°C (50°C). How long this will take depends on thickness of salmon pieces; estimate between 10–20 minutes.

Meanwhile, in a large frying pan, melt butter. Stir in leeks, add remainder of salt, and sauté, stirring occasionally, for about 5 minutes, until leeks have wilted and begun to brown in parts.

Remove leeks to a serving plate, and top with salmon pieces. Garnish with lemon quarters.

Fried Trout & Sweet Potato Stamppot

· MAKES 4 SERVINGS ·

You do not have to make this with trout; it works similarly well with salmon or grouper—really, any fish you can commonly find in steaks. I cut the trout Nick brings home from fishing trips into steaks, give it a sweet, gingery marinade, and serve it over a stamppot of sweet potatoes and broccoli for a cheap, flavorful, reasonably healthy weeknight dinner.

4 tbsp ketjap manis, divided

1 tbsp finely grated fresh ginger

1 tbsp sesame oil

1 lemon, zest and juice

½ tsp ground black pepper

3 lb (1.4 kg) whole trout, cut into 1.5-in (4-cm) steaks or 4–6 pre-cut trout steaks

1 lb (454 g) orange-fleshed sweet potatoes, peeled and diced

½ lb (250 g) broccoli, stalks separated and roughly chopped, florets trimmed into bite-sized pieces

2 tbsp canola or other neutral oil

¼ cup (60 mL) butter

1 large navel orange, zest and juice

1 green onion, minced

In a bowl, combine 2 tbsp ketjap manis, ginger, sesame oil, lemon zest and juice, and pepper. Place fish steaks into a large freezer bag, and pour marinade over top. Gently squish marinade around to coat fish, then seal tightly. Marinate for 30 minutes.

Preheat oven to 350°F (175°C).

Place sweet potatoes in a large pot of cold salted water. Bring to a boil on medium-high heat, and boil for 5 minutes. Add broccoli stalks, and cook for another 5 minutes, or until sweet potatoes and stalks are tender. Add broccoli florets, and cook for another 2 minutes.

Meanwhile, in a frying pan on high, heat oil. Cook trout steaks for about 3 minutes, until trout lifts easily from the pan. Flip, then transfer to oven and bake for 10–12 minutes, until fish flakes easily with a fork.

Drain broccoli and sweet potatoes. Add butter to warm pot and let melt before returning drained vegetables to pot. Mash vegetables into melted butter, leaving chunky bits of sweet potatoes and broccoli for texture. Stir in orange zest and juice, then spoon out onto a platter.

Place cooked trout steaks on mash. Drizzle with remainder of ketjap manis and sprinkle with minced green onions. Serve hot.

Braised Meatballs

I will admit these are not exactly traditional Dutch meatballs, but they are our Dutch meatballs. One day we didn't have any stock but we had beer, and we didn't have some other thing so we subbed something else and eventually they morphed into these, which are a lot like the Indonesian-inspired meatballs one might find in the Netherlands, and we're all pretty happy with them. Serve with Hutspot (p. 179) or on buns.

Tip: Leftover meatballs are delicious sliced and served cold in sandwiches with mayonnaise, yellow mustard, and dill pickles.

2 lb (900 g) lean ground beef

½ cup (125 mL) bread crumbs

1 egg

4 garlic cloves, minced

2 green onions, finely chopped

1 tbsp Maggi

1 tsp grainy Dijon or Dutch mustard

½ tsp ground nutmeg

½ tsp ground black pepper

1 tbsp butter

1 onion, halved lengthwise and thinly sliced

1 tbsp all-purpose flour

1 12-oz (341-mL) bottle lager or pilsner beer

¼ cup (125 mL) ketjap manis

2 tsp apple cider vinegar

salt and pepper, to taste

In a large bowl, mix ground beef, bread crumbs, egg, garlic, green onions, Maggi, mustard, nutmeg, and pepper until thoroughly combined. Form into 12 meatballs. Set aside.

In a large pan on medium-high heat, melt butter. Working in batches, brown meatballs on top and bottom, remove from pan, and set aside.

Add onions to pan, stir to coat in fat, and sprinkle in flour. Stir to combine. Reduce heat to medium-low, and deglaze pan with beer, scraping bottom of pan to catch any tasty browned bits. Stir in ketjap manis and apple cider vinegar, then return all meatballs to pan. Cover and simmer meatballs for about 40 minutes.

Adjust seasonings to taste, then serve hot straight from the pan.

Captain's Dinner with Two Peas & Yellow Cauliflower

·· MAKES 4 SERVINGS ··

This is something Dutch sea captains would eat on their voyages to the East Indies. (It's also called kapucijnerschotel, and I am not going to attempt to say that.) Traditionally, this dish would be a hash of meat and kapucijners, a particular variety of pea that's not widely available outside of the Netherlands. Here, we use chickpeas and frozen green peas instead. Serve over rice and, on the side, an assortment of pickles, mustard and, if you're so inclined, hot sauce.

4 strips regular-sliced bacon, cut into lardons

1 onion, finely chopped

3 garlic cloves, minced

1 lb (454 g) lean ground beef

2 tbsp tomato paste

1 tsp ground cumin

½ tsp ground black pepper

½ tsp kosher salt

14-oz (398-mL) can chickpeas, drained and rinsed

salt and pepper, to taste

1 medium cauliflower, trimmed and cut into florets

2 tbsp butter

1 tbsp lemon juice

1 tsp grainy Dijon mustard

1 tsp yellow curry powder

⅛ tsp ground turmeric

½ cup (125 mL) frozen peas

kosher salt, to taste

In a large pot on medium-high heat, cook bacon until crisp and most of the fat has rendered out. Remove from pot to a plate lined with paper towel and set aside. Drain off all but 2 tbsp fat.

Add onions to pot and sauté for about 4 minutes, until lightly browned. Reduce heat to medium. Add garlic and sauté for 1 minute, until golden. Add beef, breaking apart with a wooden spoon, and cook for about 8 minutes, until browned.

Stir in tomato paste, cumin, pepper, and salt, and mix to combine thoroughly. Cook until tomato paste begins to stick to bottom of pot, then add ½ cup (125 mL) water. Add chickpeas, and return bacon to pot. Simmer for about 3 minutes, until most of the water has evaporated. Adjust seasonings to taste. Meanwhile, in a pot fitted with a steamer basket, steam cauliflower in about ½ cup (125 mL) lightly salted water for 4 minutes. Drain cauliflower and set aside.

Return pot to stove on medium heat. In a small bowl, whisk together butter, lemon juice, mustard, curry powder, and turmeric. Add to pot. Add cauliflower to pot, and toss to coat in butter mixture. Just before serving, add frozen peas to beef mixture and cook until just warmed through, about 1 minute.

Sprinkle cauliflower with kosher salt, and serve alongside meat and pea hash.

Dutch Macaroni

This is straight-up "I have to feed these hungry kids immediately" food, and since mine appreciates it, I bet yours will too. It reminds me of a cross between American goulash—or Hamburger Helper—and the "pasta with meat sauce" everyone's mom in the suburbs always made. It's a hearty, easy, and satisfying one-pot meal—and it's a regular feature on Dutch dinner tables for good reason.

1 lb (454 g) lean ground beef

1 tsp kosher salt

1 tbsp olive oil

1 onion, diced

1 red bell pepper, diced

2 carrots, peeled and diced

2 celery stalks, diced

3 garlic cloves, roughly chopped

6-oz (156-mL) can low-sodium or no-salt-added tomato paste

1 tbsp Worcestershire sauce

1 tsp grainy Dijon or Dutch mustard

1 tsp ground black pepper

½ tsp smoked paprika

½ tsp dried oregano

½ tsp dried basil

14 oz (398 g) dry macaroni

4 cups (1 L) low-sodium or homemade chicken stock

4 oz (125 g) shredded Edam cheese

In a large pot on medium, brown beef with salt in olive oil for about 5 minutes. Remove meat from pot and set aside. Drain off all but 2 tbsp grease.

Add onions, bell peppers, carrots, celery, and garlic, and sauté for about 4 minutes, until colors have brightened and vegetables are shiny. Stir in tomato paste, Worcestershire sauce, mustard, pepper, smoked paprika, oregano, and basil, and coat vegetables.

Return beef to pot. Add macaroni, and stir well. Add chicken stock; liquid should just cover mixture. If not, add 1–2 cups (250–500 mL) water.

Bring contents to a simmer, and cook 10–12 minutes, until macaroni is tender.

Add Edam and stir until melted. Serve immediately.

Braised Endive with Bacon & Mustard Sauce

I have served this as a side dish with a bit of roast chicken and it's superb, but it's also lovely for breakfast, topped with a poached egg; for breakfast (or breakfast for dinner), it makes enough for two or three people. Braising the endives until tender but not mushy brings out their natural sweetness; pick them up in November, at the peak of their growing season.

4 slices bacon, trimmed into
    lardons
4–6 Belgian endives, trimmed
    and halved lengthwise
2 cups (500 mL) low-sodium or
    homemade chicken stock
1 garlic clove, smashed
1 thyme sprig
1 tsp grainy Dijon mustard
2 tsp lemon juice
3 tbsp cold butter
salt and pepper, to taste

In a large frying pan on medium heat, sauté bacon for about 6 minutes, until crisp and most of the fat has rendered out, stirring frequently. Remove cooked bacon to a plate lined with paper towels, and set aside. Pour out all but 2 tbsp fat.

Nestle endive halves in pan, cut-side down, and cook, uncovered, for 3 minutes, until crisp and golden, with the occasional charred bit. Gently turn over, cut-side up.

Add chicken stock, garlic clove, and thyme. Cover pan and cook for 10 minutes.

Gently remove endives from pan and lay out on a serving dish. Remove thyme sprig and garlic clove and discard.

Turn heat up to medium-high. Whisk in mustard and lemon juice. Cook for about 1 minute, then, 1 tbsp at a time, add butter, whisking constantly until it has melted into sauce. Return bacon to pan. Taste and adjust seasonings as needed. Pour sauce over endives.

Hot Lightning

Traditionally, hete bliksem ("hot lightning") is a mash of potatoes and apples with bacon and onions. In its most recognizable form, it's certainly delicious, but there are only so many mashes I can pass off as dinner before the boys begin to revolt. In this version, it's reimagined as a kind of warm potato and apple salad, which I serve with sausages.

4 slices bacon, finely chopped

1 lb (454 g) crisp, sweet apples, such as Honeycrisp or Ambrosia

1 lb (454 g) new or nugget potatoes, scrubbed and cut into quarters

½ tsp kosher salt

½ cup (125 mL) apple cider or unsweetened apple juice

2 tbsp fancy molasses

¼ tsp ground allspice

¼ tsp ground black pepper

1 tsp apple cider vinegar

½ tsp grainy mustard

1 tsp chopped fresh thyme

2 green onions, finely chopped

Preheat oven to 375°F (190ºC).

In a 12-in (30-cm) cast-iron pan on medium-high heat, cook bacon for about 6 minutes, until crispy and all the fat has rendered out. Remove bacon from pan, place on a plate lined with paper towels, and set aside. Drain all but 3 tbsp fat from pan. (If not enough fat, add olive oil to make 3 tbsp.)

Core and quarter apples. Halve each quarter lengthwise, then halve again crosswise. Add apples and potatoes to pan, sprinkle with salt, and toss to coat.

Roast apples and potatoes for 60 minutes, turning pieces over after 30 minutes.

After apple-potato mixture has roasted for about 50 minutes, in a small saucepan on medium-high, combine apple juice, molasses, allspice, and pepper. Bring to a simmer and cook, stirring frequently, until reduced by about half—it should be about the consistency of maple syrup. Add cider vinegar and mustard, and set aside.

Remove potato and apple mixture from oven. Sprinkle with thyme and reserved bacon, then pour apple juice reduction over top, stirring to coat. Serve in pan or spooned onto a serving plate, and garnish with chopped green onions.

Bums in the Grass

Also known as "Blote Billetjes In Het Groen." The naming here is pretty straightforward—this looks like naked bums frolicking in fields of grass, kind of. Really pale bums. Is this recipe about me? Anyway, this is a hearty side dish and works well as an accompaniment to sausages or grilled fish—it's also good cold with a squeeze of lemon if you want to eat the leftovers as a salad the next day.

19-oz (540-mL) can white
    kidney beans
1 lb (454 g) green beans,
    trimmed
4 green onions
3 tbsp butter
salt, to taste
1/8 tsp ground nutmeg

Drain and rinse canned beans. Set aside.

Slice green beans on the diagonal, so that each slice is pointy at the top and bottom. Slice green onions on the diagonal as well. (Green beans and onions are meant to resemble blades of grass.)

Bring a large pot of salted water on high heat to a boil. Fill a large bowl with ice water and set aside.

Add green beans to boiling water, and cook for 30 seconds. Drain and plunge into ice water. Once cool, drain and pat dry.

In a large pan on medium-high, melt butter. Add green onions, green beans, and canned beans, and cook for 4–6 minutes, until green beans are glossy and white beans are warmed through. Taste and adjust seasonings as needed—canned beans can be salty enough.

Sprinkle with nutmeg to serve.

Sugar Snap Peas with Herb Vinaigrette

This is a great way to make something a little different with all the peas and herbs in your garden (or, if you're like me, all the peas and herbs you bought on sale and then forgot about before buying a whole bunch more). It's a bright, crunchy salad with a natural sweetness that compliments rich main dishes. I make this all summer long.

¼ cup (60 mL) olive oil

2 tbsp fresh lime juice

1 tsp honey

½ tsp kosher salt

½ tsp ground black pepper

¼ tsp ground coriander

1 lb (454 g) sugar snap peas, trimmed

4 green onions, thinly sliced on the diagonal

¼ cup (60 mL) finely chopped fresh mint

¼ cup (60 mL) finely chopped fresh cilantro

In a large bowl, whisk together oil, juice, honey, salt, pepper, and coriander. Taste and adjust seasonings as needed.

Bring a pot of salted water on high heat to a boil. Fill a large bowl with ice cold water and set aside.

Add snap peas to boiling water, and cook for 1 minute. Drain, then add peas to ice water. Cool completely, then strain again and pat dry.

Add peas, green onions, mint, and cilantro to bowl with vinaigrette, and toss to coat.

These can be made up to 30 minutes ahead; store in refrigerator until ready to serve.

Cucumber Salad

We eat this a lot because it's the easiest thing in the world, cucumbers are often on sale, it goes with just about everything, and it's endlessly adaptable. While the recipe calls for yogurt, I've made it with milk kefir, sour cream, and buttermilk—all with great results. Use whatever herbs you like—I like a combination of dill and cilantro.

1 long English cucumber
1 shallot
1 tsp kosher salt
3 tbsp plain yogurt
½ tsp ground black pepper
2 tbsp chopped fresh dill
2 tbsp chopped fresh cilantro

Using a mandoline or very sharp knife, cut cucumber and shallot into thin rounds. Place in a colander in sink, sprinkle with salt, and crush mixture with your hands to release liquid. Let this rest for about 30 minutes, then press out any remaining liquid.

Move cucumber-shallot mixture to a bowl, then mix in yogurt and pepper. Refrigerate for up to an hour.

Before serving, mix in dill and cilantro, reserving a couple of pinches to sprinkle over top.

Celery Salad

The Dutch cookbook *De Verstandige Kock* (published in 1667) contains just a few recipes for raw vegetable salads, though there is a simple recipe for celery salad. I intended to leave it as it was, dressed in oil and vinegar with a little pepper and salt, but it needed an herb or two, and then I added an apple and some fennel seeds. I feel like it's still an homage, but perhaps a modern one. If you are lucky enough to find celery with leaves still attached, pluck them off the stalks and serve in this salad as an herb.

1½ tsp fennel seeds

2 tbsp olive oil

1 tbsp white wine vinegar

½ tsp kosher salt

½ tsp ground black pepper

6 celery stalks, rinsed and trimmed

1 tart, green apple, such as Granny Smith

1 tbsp minced fresh tarragon

⅓ cup fresh flat-leaf parsley, stems discarded

In a saucepan on medium-high heat, fry fennel seeds in olive oil until golden, about 2 minutes. Scrape oil and seeds pan into a large bowl, and set aside to cool completely.

Whisk vinegar, salt, and pepper into fennel seeds in oil.

Core apple and halve lengthwise, then slice thinly. Slice celery stalks thinly, on the diagonal. Add apple, celery, tarragon, and parsley leaves, plus celery leaves if you have them, to dressing, and toss to coat.

Refrigerate for up to 30 minutes before serving.

Beppe Slaw

Iceberg lettuce is good stuff; I don't care what anyone thinks. It may not be trendy but it's cheap and it feeds a lot of people, and it's not so delicate it can't withstand a mayonnaise-based dressing and a short rest in the fridge before dinner. Maybe that's why Nick's grandmother Beppe and his mom make it. I ask for it on my birthday.

1 head iceberg lettuce

½ onion, thinly sliced

2 hard-boiled eggs

¼ cup (60 mL) mayonnaise

1 tbsp white vinegar

1 tsp granulated sugar

salt, to taste

2 green onions, thinly sliced

Halve lettuce lengthwise and cut out core. Halve each half again lengthwise, then cut lettuce crosswise into thin ribbons, and place into a large salad bowl. Add thinly sliced onions.

Cut hard-boiled eggs crosswise into rounds.

In a small bowl, mix mayonnaise, vinegar, sugar, and salt.

Dress lettuce and onions with mayonnaise mixture, tossing to coat. Garnish with egg slices and green onions.

Beer

I spent many an hour just idling in Haarlem and Rotterdam as Nick chose exactly the right beer to brag to his friend Greg Rinsma about, or selecting from a limited number of Dutch brewery-brand beer glasses to show off to Greg, which Nick would somehow have to carry home on a plane without shattering. He bought four, and they all made it home, and I don't have room to store anything because we have at least two dozen mismatched beer glasses that take up a lot of space.

What I am saying is that maybe there's a beer gene, and the VanderWouds and Rinsmas of the world carry it on the dominant allele. Also, beer can be a competition if you get the right apps on your phone.

The Dutch are a beer-loving people; during the Middle Ages, each city in the Netherlands had its own brewery, and at its peak in the eighteenth century, the Netherlands had 700 breweries. For a long time, beer was the most popular drink after water, commonly consumed as part of a hearty breakfast. Today, there are around 320 breweries in the country. Most of the beer production—primarily of pale beers like pilsner and lager—is dominated by Heineken, Grolsch, and Bavaria. On average, the Dutch consume around sixty-eight liters (eighteen gallons) of beer per person per year; Americans drink around seventy-six liters (twenty gallons) per person per year, much of it possibly exported by Dutch brewers. As much as fifty percent of beer produced in the Netherlands is for export. Perhaps inspired by the craft beer revolution taking place around the world, smaller breweries have begun looking to older styles of beer, and many are heavily influenced by traditional Belgian beers.

Beer is for drinking, but it is also an essential aspect of Dutch cuisine; it's used in a wide range of recipes, from soups and stews to bierpap, a kind of porridge made of milk and beer, thickened with flour and lightly sweetened. According to the author of the blog The Dutch Table, it's the kind of thing you might take as a nightcap. I'll trust her on this one.

A modern challenge inherent in cooking with beer is that it is popular to add distinctive hop notes to beers; this is fine for drinking, but in many recipes, hoppy beers can disrupt the balance of flavors you worked so hard to carefully craft, or otherwise throw a dish right off. (Unpopular opinion time: I think a lot of really hoppy beers taste like earwax. Don't ask me how I know.) A mild pilsner or lager will work well with most dishes but especially seafood, especially mussels; red and amber ales have a more malty taste that adds rich flavor and a sort of breadiness that compliments stews and braises. Some dishes call for a darker beer, such as a porter or stout (in cooking, you can use these interchangeably), and I select as much for color as for flavor, as both yield an earthy, smoky taste and a deep, appetizing color. Brown food is good food, always.

To accompany food, many people choose rich Belgian or Belgian-style beers; some of these are more like wine—they have as much complexity and depth of flavor as any wine. Nick's preference in the Netherlands was for De Koningshoeven, a Dutch brewery that's one of just a handful of Trappist-style breweries outside of Belgium that make a variety of traditional and strong beers. Because of their distinctive character, these pair well with borrels, especially cured meats and cheeses, or Cheese Cookies (p. 92), or with hearty meals such as Keeshi Yena (p. 112) or Dutch Macaroni (p. 125).

As when cooking with wine, it's best to drink the same or similar variety as that used in the recipe. Belgian and Trappist-style beers can be expensive, so I do not recommend cooking with them unless you have a very specific reason or recipe—the recipes in this book do not require this. As with wine, use a beer you would happily drink, but that is not prohibitively expensive. We don't waste beer. Nick and Greg would not approve.

RIJSTTAFEL (RICE TABLE)

SAOTO
144

YELLOW RICE
146

MAGGI FRIED RICE
147

NASI GORENG WITH TEMPEH
148

BAMI GORENG
150

MUSSELS WITH BEER &
RED CHILIES
151

GADO GADO
153

CHICKEN SATE
154

TEMPEH WITH
TOMATOES & EGGPLANT
156

CHICKEN LIVER CURRY
158

FRIED PLANTAINS
159

SPICY PRAWNS
WITH GREEN BEANS
160

MEATBALL CURRY
162

BABI KETJAP
164

BANANA ICE CREAM
165

SALTED LICORICE ICE CREAM
168

RIJSTTAFEL
(RICE TABLE)

You can't really talk about Dutch food without talking about Indonesia. And you can't really talk about the Dutch in Indonesia without talking about race and the role of white, western perspectives on the way we interpret our history. We tend to selectively remember our past, and we tend to omit the unpleasantness we have been responsible for from our collective memory. While history books—and textbooks in particular—have a way of glossing over the gritty bits, making the story of European conquest seem like an adventurous pursuit of progress, the truth is never so easily digestible. We have taken things that were never ours and then not taken responsibility for the consequences.

Nowhere is this absence of memory more apparent than in cookbooks and in the way we talk about food. Food is deeply, intensely personal, and we lay claim to certain dishes or cuisines because flavor satisfies something elemental in each of us. When we make a recipe and it becomes a part of our family's culinary repertoire, that recipe is ours. For most people, food does not exist to sate physical hunger alone—even if we mostly eat to live, all of us occasionally eat to cozy up to a feeling we're chasing, whether that's comfort or memory or longing. A lot of times, when the people who write cookbooks talk about food and place, it is in that idealized, hazy way in which you view a place or a dish in a very limited context, as if through sunglasses. We write about the way things make us feel because we want you to feel the same way. Food is love! Sharing is caring! But how did we get those recipes, and what happened before we got to experience them?

For example, how did the Dutch get rijsttafel? Let's just say it wasn't a fun dinner party to which the Dutch were invited guests.

Dutch merchants, craving spices, arrived in Indonesia in 1595. Prior to the European colonial age that began in the fifteenth century, flavors were largely vegetal, with herbs and flowers used to enhance the meats, seafood, and vegetables available at the time. In pre-colonial Dutch recipes, rose water was used often in sweet dishes and baking, a flavoring that would later be replaced by vanilla. Once they found out about spices, they were hooked. And like the British, French, and Portuguese, when they realized that they could sell what they bought in Asia for a premium in Europe, more merchants and traders wanted in, and soon enterprising colonizers sought to bring Indonesia under Dutch hegemony, which was never especially popular with the people who lived there first, as is the way with these kinds of things. When we talk about Indonesia in the context of Dutch cuisine, what we are often talking about is Indo-Dutch cuisine, which is different.

The Dutch occupied Indonesia for 350 years, and during that time they came to love the local cuisine, and like colonials everywhere, wanted to share a taste of "the exotic" with friends and family. Unfortunately, they weren't just there for the food; as they were falling madly in love with all things goreng, they were also there to extract resources and boost a strong economy back home. Dutch occupation of Indonesia was an ongoing and, at times, a violent process—the Dutch military was met with considerable resistance—and expansion of Dutch power in the region resulted in a number of bloody, years-long wars against indigenous groups.

During World War II, when the Japanese initially arrived in Indonesia, they were welcomed as liberators, defeating the Dutch and gaining control of the country for nearly five years. But when the axis forces were defeated and the war ended in 1945, the Dutch tried to take back the country. After the Japanese surrendered in 1945—and after four million Indonesians died in the interim—Indonesia declared independence. When the Dutch returned to reclaim Indonesia, they faced a lengthy struggle against guerrilla forces who did not want them there, and ultimately succumbed to pressure (both in Indonesia and internationally) to relinquish whatever claim they might have had and returned Indonesia to its people in 1949.

You can see the influence of Indonesia wherever there are Dutch people, including in Suriname and the Caribbean, where the Dutch brought indentured workers from Java to Suriname after slavery in that country ended in 1873. Indentured servitude was a way to recruit workers cheaply, and was itself a form of captivity used by colonial powers after slavery was abolished, particularly in the Caribbean, where economies relied on sugar and cotton and needed inexpensive bodies to work the plantations. Colonialism was not a feel-good story by any stretch, but a side-effect was that people moved around a fair bit and left a lasting impression on their new homelands.

Following the end of Dutch occupation, the Netherlands saw an increase in immigration from Indonesia, with many of those immigrants doing what people new to a place do: they established businesses, and they opened restaurants. To this day, some of the best food in the Netherlands is Indonesian or Indo-Dutch cuisine. Many Indonesian restaurants throughout the country still serve rijsttafel, and Dutch versions of Indonesian condiments are widely available. Today, there are more than 400,000 people of Indonesian descent who are first or second-generation Dutch citizens; the relationship between the Netherlands and Indonesia is now a partnership, with strong economic ties.

Rijsttafel is to Indonesia as Chicken Tikka Masala is to Britain, which is to say that it is a Dutch interpretation of Indonesian food. Rijsttafel translates as "rice table." It showcases a variety of Indonesian dishes to which the Dutch were exposed and became enamored with. It is an elaborate feast, sometimes made with dozens

of little dishes accompanied by rice. For the early colonizers, it was meant to be shared with European guests in a display of "exoticism" and wealth. Now, dishes like Bami Goreng and Babi Ketjap can easily be ordered in or made at home in any well-stocked kitchen.

Modern rijsttafel can include any number or combination of dishes, but I find that six main dishes plus rice and condiments (store-bought is totally fine)—and dessert, of course—is plenty when cooking and entertaining at home. (The last time we had rijsttafel, eight guests and thirteen dishes dirtied every last one of my plates, bowls, and platters, and most of my cutlery as well.) With Dutch sensibility in mind, I suggest never making more than you have the energy to tidy up after everyone's gone home. Two dishes plus rice makes a lovely treat some evening when it's just you and your family.

And know that when you make these dishes, they are yours. And when you think about Indonesia and those tropical flavors that feel so different from what you might be used to, remember how those recipes came to be Dutch first. The relationships and struggles behind what we eat are so interesting, I think, and the way we eat can change how we see the world.

Saoto

MAKES 4–6 SERVINGS AS A MAIN DISH, OR 8 AS A STARTER

Saoto is a brothy, citrusy chicken soup from Suriname via Indonesia, and it is customarily served as the first course in a rice table feast. This is what my son Hunter refers to as "good broth," the sort of nourishing, fragrant dish that is nice at the start of a feast but also perfect for a rainy day when everyone in your home has a bit of a cold. Pairs well with mint tea or ice-cold gin with a squirt of lime.

SOUP

3–4 lb (1.3–1.8 kg) whole chicken
1 large sweet onion, trimmed and halved
1 garlic head, halved crosswise
3-in (7.5-cm) piece ginger, peeled and sliced
1 tbsp kosher salt
1 tbsp coriander seeds
2 tsp cumin seeds
1 tsp black peppercorns
6 fresh or frozen makrut lime leaves
1 lemongrass stalk, trimmed and halved lengthwise
1 celery stalk, cut into 3 pieces
2 tbsp fish sauce
1 tbsp granulated sugar
1 tsp ground turmeric
1 lime, juiced
7–10 oz (200–300 g) rice vermicelli
2 cups (500 mL) fresh bean sprouts
4 green onions, finely chopped
4 Thai bird or other hot chilies, finely chopped

ACCOMPANIMENTS

4–6 hard-boiled eggs, peeled and halved
celery leaves
sambal oelek or other chili paste
ketjap manis
lime wedges
chopped fresh cilantro

In a large pot, cover chicken with cold water. Bring pot to a boil on high heat, and cook at a rolling boil for 6 minutes. Drain chicken, and set aside. Rinse pot.

Return chicken to pot, and cover once more with cold water. Add onions, garlic, ginger, salt, coriander and cumin seeds, peppercorns, lime leaves, lemongrass, celery, fish sauce, sugar, and turmeric. On medium heat, bring to a simmer and cook for 60 minutes, reducing heat as needed to prevent liquid from boiling.

Remove chicken from pot and let cool. Continue to simmer broth until chicken is cool enough to handle, about 20 minutes. Add lime juice to broth. Taste broth and adjust seasonings as needed.

Prepare rice noodles according to package instructions.

Carve meat off chicken and slice into bite-sized pieces.

Distribute rice noodles evenly between bowls. Place a handful of bean sprouts in each bowl. Divide chicken evenly between each

Saoto cont'd

bowl. Add two halves of a hardboiled egg to each bowl. Ladle hot broth through a fine mesh strainer into each bowl.

Garnish with green onions and chopped chilies, and allow guests to customize their bowls with accompaniments.

Yellow Rice

This rice is very yellow. Not much more complicated to make than plain rice, it's a nice mix of coconut, turmeric, and ginger, but the flavor is mild—it will complement your rijsttafel (and make it more beautiful) without taking away from the main dishes. The next day—if there's any left over—yellow rice is delicious fried with chopped leftover Babi Ketjap (page 164), a handful of cilantro, and a couple of eggs.

1 cup (250 mL) long-grain
    white rice
2 tbsp butter
1 tbsp minced fresh ginger
1/3 cup (80 mL) medium
    shredded coconut
    (unsweetened)
1 cup (250 mL) coconut milk
1½ tsp ground turmeric
1 tsp kosher salt

Place rice in a fine mesh strainer and rinse with cold water until water runs clear, working rice with your fingers to thoroughly rinse grains. Set aside.

In a saucepan with a tight-fitting lid on medium-high heat, melt butter. Add ginger, and sauté for about 1 minute. Add coconut, stirring frequently to prevent scorching, and cook for about 1 minute. Add coconut milk, scraping bottom of pan.

Add turmeric, salt, rice, and 1 cup (250 mL) cold water, and bring to a boil. Cover with lid and reduce heat to low. Cook for 20 minutes.

Remove from heat. Let rice sit, still covered, for 5 minutes. Fluff with a fork to loosen the grains before serving.

Maggi Fried Rice

MAKES 4–6 SERVINGS

This umami-rich side dish works well with the fresh, bright flavors of Gado Gado (p.153), Chicken Sate (p.154), and Mussels with Beer & Red Chilies (p. 151). It's also a way to trick a kid into eating mushrooms because, if they're young enough, they'll think the mushrooms are meat—not that I would ever do that. Never. But, you know.

2 shallots, finely chopped

½ lb (250 g) mushrooms, roughly chopped

3 tbsp canola or other neutral oil, divided

½ tsp ground cumin

½ tsp ground black pepper

3 cups cooked long-grain white rice

2 tbsp Maggi

1 tsp sesame oil

In a frying pan on medium-high heat, sauté shallots and mushrooms in 1 tbsp canola oil for about 6 minutes, until mushrooms have softened, released their liquid, and shrunk in volume. Add cumin and pepper, and cook until mushrooms begin to brown and caramelize, another 2–3 minutes.

Add rice to pan, breaking it up as needed with a wooden spoon. Stir to mix mushrooms and rice well, and cook until the rice has warmed through, about 2 minutes.

Stir in Maggi and sesame oil, mix well, then transfer to a serving dish.

Nasi Goreng with Tempeh

This dish is the stuff of crisper scraps and leftovers. If you can't find tempeh, some of yesterday's roast chicken will work just as well. I like it with tempeh as it's a vegetarian protein I can sneak into my son Hunter; the finely chopped veggies in this are also easy to put past him, so it ends up being a healthy meal that he accepts without complaint. Serve with sliced avocado, sambal oelek, chopped peanuts, and a fried egg for a filling, satisfying vegetarian dinner.

2 tbsp ketjap manis

2 tbsp sambal oelek

1 tbsp sesame oil

1 tbsp creamy peanut butter

1 lime, zest and juice

2 tsp ground cumin

½ tsp ground turmeric

½ tsp ground coriander

½ tsp ground black pepper

3 tbsp canola or other neutral oil

1 tbsp minced fresh ginger

1 shallot, minced

4 garlic cloves, minced

7-oz (200-g) block tempeh, finely chopped

2 cups finely chopped carrots

1 tbsp soy sauce

1 tbsp tomato paste

2 cups finely chopped green beans

4 green onions, white and light-green / dark-green parts divided

1 red bell pepper, finely chopped

1 celery stalk, finely chopped

3 cups (750 mL) cooked long-grain white rice

salt and pepper, to taste

chopped fresh cilantro, for garnish

In a small bowl, whisk together ketjap manis, sambal oelek, sesame oil, peanut butter, lime zest and juice, cumin, turmeric, coriander, and black pepper. Set aside.

In a large pan on medium-high, heat oil. Sauté ginger, shallots, and garlic for about 2 minutes, until just beginning to brown. Add tempeh, carrots, soy sauce, and tomato paste, and sauté for 2 minutes, until tempeh and carrots begin to brown and liquids begin to stick to pan. Add green beans, white part of green onions, bell peppers, celery, and ¼ cup (60 mL) water. Scrape bottom of the pan to release solids, and stir to coat vegetables. Cook for about 3 minutes, until vegetables have softened a bit.

Stir in rice to incorporate well. Add ketjap manis mixture and stir until thoroughly incorporated.

Taste and adjust seasonings as needed. Just before serving, stir in finely chopped light and dark green parts of green onions and fresh cilantro.

Tempeh

Bami Goreng

My favorite thing about the Surinamese version of bami goreng, an Indonesian fried noodle dish, is that it uses spaghetti noodles. It's the ultimate "quick, what do we have in the cupboard?" kind of dish, and if you're throwing it together for an easy weeknight dinner, it's great garnished with a fried egg and some cubed avocado. If you don't eat peanuts, use cashews instead. Use tongs to stir (and serve) for best results.

13 oz (375 g) spaghetti noodles

2 tbsp canola or other neutral oil

1 tbsp minced fresh ginger

2 garlic cloves, minced

1 onion, halved and thinly sliced

1 red bell pepper, thinly sliced

¼ cup (60 mL) ketjap manis

1 cup (250 mL) bean sprouts

2 tsp sesame oil

1½ tsp yellow curry powder

½ tsp ground black pepper

½ cup (125 mL) chopped roasted peanuts

2 green onions, thinly sliced

In a large pot of salted water on high, cook noodles until al dente. Before draining, reserve ½ cup (125 mL) cooking water.

Meanwhile, in a large pan on medium-high, heat oil. Sauté ginger and garlic for about 3 minutes, until just beginning to brown. Add onions and bell peppers, and cook for 2 minutes, until just softened.

Add cooked spaghetti noodles, ketjap manis, bean sprouts, sesame oil, curry powder, and pepper. Stir to combine. Add reserved cooking water, and mix again to coat noodles in sauce. Cook another 3 minutes, until liquid has reduced and sauce coats noodles and vegetables.

Taste and adjust seasonings as needed. Top with roasted peanuts and green onions.

Mussels with Beer & Red Chilies

This dish practically begs for an ice-cold beer, making it a perfect rijsttafel main or side. It's great with Yellow Rice (p. 146), but it's just as good with crusty bread. Given how quick this is to cook, it's ideal for a Friday night dinner party. To save time, look for farmed mussels, which are often cleaner and beard-free.

2.2 lb (1 kg) fresh mussels, scrubbed and de-bearded

¼ cup (60 mL) butter

6 green onions, chopped

4 garlic cloves, minced

4 red chilies, such as Thai bird chilies, minced

1 tbsp lemon juice

.1 tsp kosher salt

1 cup (250 mL) lager or pilsner beer

fresh basil, for garnish

Look over mussels, discarding any that are broken or won't close when squeezed. Wash mussels and, using a clean pair of tweezers, remove beards—the hairy bits poking out from side of shell.

In a large pot on medium-high heat, melt butter. Add white and light-green parts of onions, and set aside dark-green parts for later. Add garlic and chilies, and sauté for about 1 minutes, until fragrant. Stir in lemon juice, fish sauce, and salt.

Add mussels, then pour beer over mussels. Cover with a lid and steam until mussels open, about 5 minutes.

Pour mussels and beer broth into a large serving bowl, discarding any mussels that did not open. Sprinkle with reserved dark-green onions and freshly torn leaves of basil.

Gado Gado

I have had this dish more than a few times, but my favorite version comes from my friends Dan and Dennis, who use chunks of fresh pineapple. The combination of ingredients may seem unusual, but as part of a rijsttafel feast it is cooling and refreshing. You can make the Peanut Sauce (p. 250) or use a store-bought variety. Serve with lime wedges and additional peanut sauce on the side.

7-oz (200-g) block tempeh, sliced into bite-sized pieces

1½ tbsp canola or other neutral oil, divided

2 tsp soy sauce

½ tsp yellow curry powder

2 cups (500 mL) bean sprouts

2 cups (500 mL) finely shredded Napa cabbage

½ cup (125 mL) peanut sauce

1 lime, zest and juice

½ English cucumber, thinly sliced

4 oz (115 g) green beans, trimmed and blanched

½ fresh pineapple, trimmed, cored, and cut into thin wedges, or two 8-oz (250 mL) cans chunk pineapple, drained

3 hard-boiled eggs, peeled and halved

2 jalapeño or serrano peppers, thinly sliced

½ cup (125 mL) roasted peanuts, finely chopped

2 green onions, minced

chopped cilantro, for garnish

In a bowl, toss tempeh in ½ tbsp oil with soy sauce and curry powder. In a frying pan on medium-high heat, sauté tempeh in remainder of oil for 2–3 minutes per side, until crisp and charred in places. Set aside.

In a large bowl, toss together bean sprouts and shredded cabbage with peanut sauce and lime zest and juice. Spread mixture over a large platter.

Place cucumbers on one side of platter. Place green beans, pineapple, eggs, and tempeh in separate sections so that the platter looks artful and enticing. You'll know it when you see it—you want guests to choose the bits and pieces they like, and mix the salad up on their own plates.

Scatter peppers, chopped peanuts, green onions, and cilantro over platter. Chill in the refrigerator for 30 minutes before serving.

Chicken Sate

Everyone likes chicken sate, even the pickiest of children (as I discovered one Christmas when Nick's family decided rijsttafel sounded better than plain old turkey dinner). The honey and soy sauce together have a tenderizing effect on the meat that makes both essential and, I think, preferable to ketjap manis (this one time); if serving Celiac-afflicted dinner guests, gluten-free soy sauce works perfectly well. In summer, we cook these on an outdoor grill; in any season, we enjoy these with Peanut Sauce (p.250) and Gado Gado (p.153), with sliced watermelon for dessert.

2 lb (900 g) boneless, skinless chicken thighs, cubed

¼ cup (60 mL) soy sauce

2 tbsp honey

1 tbsp sesame oil

1 garlic clove, minced

1 lime, zest and juice

2 tsp sambal oelek

½ tsp ground black pepper

Combine chicken, soy sauce, honey, sesame oil, garlic, lime zest and juice, sambal oelek, and pepper in a bowl. Use your hands to thoroughly combine ingredients and coat chicken. Cover with plastic wrap, and press down against chicken to seal. Refrigerate for 2–4 hours.

Place 16 bamboo skewers in a 9 x 13-in (3.5-L) baking dish, and cover with cold water. Soak for 30 minutes.

Thread chicken cubes onto skewers, ensuring that each has about the same amount of chicken. Press cubes against each other toward blunt end of skewer so meat stays juicy and doesn't overcook.

If cooking indoors, preheat broiler. If cooking on an outdoor grill, heat to about 400°F (200°C).

If cooking indoors, lay skewers on a foil-lined baking sheet and broil for 5–6 minutes per side (turning once), until lightly charred and cooked through. (Juices should run clear, or the internal temperature should be 165°F [75°C].)

If cooking on a grill, cook on direct heat about 4 minutes per side, until lightly charred and cooked through.

Tempeh with Tomatoes & Eggplant

······················· MAKES 4 SERVINGS ·······················

We call this dish "Indonesian-ish ratatouille," and I make it all summer long when the tomatoes are so ripe they're practically bursting and the eggplant is meaty and firm. To serve this to vegetarian or vegan friends, I sub out the fish sauce and use soy sauce instead. Make this the day before for best results.

3 tbsp canola or vegetable oil, divided

2 shallots, roughly chopped

6 garlic gloves

1-in (2.5-cm) piece ginger, peeled and sliced

1 stalk lemongrass

3 tbsp brown sugar

2 tbsp sambal oelek

1 tbsp molasses

1 tbsp fish sauce

1 tsp ground turmeric

1 lime leaf

1 lime, zest and juice

7 oz (200 g) block tempeh, cut into 1-in (2.5-cm) squares

½ lb (225 g) Japanese eggplant, halved lengthwise and cut into 1-in (2.5-cm) pieces

1½ lb (680 g) tomatoes, quartered lengthwise and then widthwise into 8 pieces

1 tsp kosher salt

½ tsp ground black pepper

½ cup (125 mL) toasted cashews

finely chopped green onions, for garnish

In a large pan on medium-high, heat 1 tbsp oil. Add shallots, garlic, ginger, and lemongrass, and sauté, stirring occasionally, for about 3 minutes, until browned and slightly charred in places. Pour mixture into a stand blender.

Add brown sugar, sambal oelek, molasses, fish sauce, turmeric, lime leaf, and lime zest and juice to blender. Blend until puréed. Set aside.

Place pan on medium-high heat and add 1 tbsp oil. Add tempeh and sauté for about 2 minutes per side, until browned and charred in places. Remove tempeh to a plate lined with paper towels.

Add final 1 tbsp oil to pan. Sauté eggplant for about 2 minutes per side, until browned and charred in places. Stir in tomatoes, and return tempeh to pan. Reduce heat to medium. Pour in sambal oelek mixture. Add salt and pepper and stir. Cook, stirring occasionally, for 10–12 minutes, until tomatoes and eggplant have released liquids and sauce has thickened. The mixture should resemble a chunky tomato sauce.

Stir cashews into pan, and sprinkle with green onions before serving.

Chicken Liver Curry

This is another quick-and-easy Friday night rijsttafel dish, and it's cheap and decadent and a good way to introduce chicken livers to those who might be new to the idea. It's a flavorful dish, and one in which the livers are the star (but not really, you know, "livery"). We had these at an Indo-Surinamese restaurant in Aruba, and I couldn't stop thinking about them—they were so rich and delicious.

1 lb (454 g) chicken livers

3 tbsp canola or other neutral oil

2 shallots, minced

4 garlic cloves, minced

1 lemongrass stalk, trimmed and finely chopped

1 tbsp minced fresh ginger

1 tbsp medium shredded coconut (unsweetened)

1 cup (250 mL) coconut cream

2 tbsp sambal oelek

1 tbsp fish sauce

1 tbsp molasses

1 tbsp brown sugar

2 tsp ground cumin

1 tsp kosher salt

½ tsp ground coriander

½ tsp ground turmeric

2 lime leaves, finely chopped

1 lime, zest and juice

salt and pepper, to taste

minced fresh chilies (optional), for garnish

cilantro leaves, torn (optional), for garnish

Trim chicken livers, removing stringy white membrane from each one. Discard membrane, and set trimmed livers aside.

In a large frying pan on high, heat oil. Add shallots, garlic, lemongrass, and ginger, and sauté for about 30 seconds, until shallots just begin to brown. Add shredded coconut and chicken livers, stirring to coat in aromatics, and cook for another minute.

Add coconut cream, sambal oelek, fish sauce, molasses, sugar, cumin, salt, coriander, turmeric, and lime leaves, and simmer for about 7 minutes, until sauce is reduced and livers are cooked through. Add lime zest and juice, adjust seasonings to taste, and pour from hot pan into a serving dish. Sprinkle with chopped chilies and cilantro if desired.

Fried Plantains

This is an easy side dish, as you can wait until about the last second to get these cooking and still have them on the table before everyone sits down. Look for plantains that look overripe and dark; these will give you the best, sweetest flavor.

2 ripe plantains, peeled and cut into 1-in (2.5-cm) pieces

6 tbsp canola or other neutral oil, divided

½ tsp kosher salt

¼ tsp ground allspice

⅛ tsp ground cinnamon

In a large bowl, toss plantains with 2 tbsp oil, salt, allspice, and cinnamon. Set aside.

In a large frying pan on medium-high, heat remainder of oil until shimmering. Working in batches, fry plantains until golden, about 2 minutes per side.

Remove plantain pieces to a plate lined with paper towels to drain excess oil. Serve hot.

Spicy Prawns with Green Beans

Green beans are a frequent side dish in Dutch cuisine; here, they're the base on which a spicy shrimp sambal rests, sopping up those good bits of garlic and chili paste. You can eat this as a standalone meal—we've done that more than a few times, with a plate of Yellow Rice (p.146)—but it's also a delicious addition to a pescatarian-friendly rijsttafel.

¼ cup (60 mL) butter

4 garlic cloves, minced

¼ cup (60 mL) sambal oelek

1 tbsp fish sauce

1 tbsp brown sugar, packed

½ tsp ground black pepper

1 lb (454 g) jumbo prawns (21–30 count), peeled and deveined

1 lb (454 g) green beans, trimmed

1 lime, zest and juice

salt, to taste

2 green onions, minced

In a large frying pan on medium-high heat, melt butter. Add garlic, and sauté for about 1 minute, until fragrant but not brown, stirring frequently. Add sambal oelek, fish sauce, brown sugar, and pepper, and cook 1–2 minutes, until liquid has mostly evaporated, leaving a chunky paste behind.

Add prawns to paste, tossing to coat, and sauté for about 4 minutes, until just cooked through.

Meanwhile, bring a large pot of salted water to a boil on high heat. Add beans, and cook for 30 seconds, until just tender. Drain and spread green beans on a platter.

Stir lime zest and juice into prawn mixture. Taste and adjust seasonings as needed. Spoon prawns over green beans. Using a spatula, scrape any remaining chili sauce from pan over top of prawns.

Sprinkle with green onions.

Meatball Curry

The ingredient list is long, but the actual work of the dish is quick and straightforward. Best made a day or two before you intend to serve it, this will provide a complex, interesting element to your rijsttafel feast, but it will also stand alone quite nicely. Nick likes this curry with Maggi and additional sambal oelek, while I like to throw a handful of chopped fresh chilies onto mine. Whether you offer these meatballs as part of a larger meal or on their own, serve with rice.

1 lb (454 g) lean ground pork
½ cup (125 mL) bread crumbs
1 egg
2 tbsp ketjap manis
1 tbsp sesame oil
3 green onions, minced
2 + 4 garlic cloves, minced and divided
3 tbsp canola oil
2 shallots, minced
2 tbsp minced fresh ginger
2 tsp ground cumin
1 tsp ground turmeric
½ tsp ground coriander
½ tsp ground black pepper
¼ tsp ground allspice
3 tsp kosher salt, divided
2 14-oz (398-mL) cans coconut milk
3 tbsp brown sugar
1 tbsp fish sauce
1 tbsp sambal oelek
4 fresh or frozen lime leaves
2 whole star anise
1 cinnamon stick
1 stalk lemongrass, trimmed and bruised

1 lime, juiced
1 cup (250 mL) frozen green peas
½ cup (125 mL) fresh cilantro, roughly chopped

In a large bowl, mix pork, bread crumbs, egg, ketjap manis, sesame oil, green onions, and 2 minced garlic cloves together with your hands. Form 18 meatballs.

In a Dutch oven on medium-high, heat oil. Brown meatballs in batches, for about 4 minutes per side. Remove meatballs to a plate, and set aside.

Reduce heat to medium. Add shallots, ginger, and remaining garlic and sauté for about 2 minutes, until just browned. Working quickly, add cumin, turmeric, coriander, pepper, allspice, and remainder of salt, and stir to coat in spices.

Stir in coconut milk, brown sugar, fish sauce, sambal oelek, lime leaves, star anise, cinnamon stick, and lemongrass. Simmer, uncovered, for 30 minutes.

Just before serving, add lime juice. Taste and adjust seasonings as needed.

Meatball Curry cont'd

If serving this right away, remove lime leaves, star anise, and lemongrass and stir in green peas and cilantro. If storing in refrigerator to serve the next day, remove lime leaves, star anise, and lemongrass before reheating. When reheated, add peas and cilantro.

Babi Ketjap

This dish is deeply satisfying, hitting all the right notes—sweet, salty, a little tart, a little smoky—best enjoyed in a bowl with a heap of white rice. It's pure Indo-Dutch comfort food, as tasty as part of a rijsttafel as it is on its own, eaten cold from the fridge after everyone else has gone to bed.

4 tbsp canola or other neutral oil, divided

2 lb (900 g) pork tenderloin, cubed

2 shallots, minced

2 tbsp minced fresh ginger

6 garlic cloves, smashed

1 serrano chili pepper, minced

½ cup (125 mL) ketjap manis

2 tbsp molasses

1 tbsp + 1 tsp lemon juice (about 1 lemon)

2 whole star anise

1 tsp ground black pepper

ACCOMPANIMENTS
sambal oelek
minced green onions
chopped red chilies
chopped roasted peanuts

In a frying pan on medium-high, heat 1 tbsp oil. Working in batches, brown pork, adding 1 tbsp oil between batches as needed, up to 3 tbsp. Remove pork to a bowl and set aside.

Add final 1 tbsp oil, and sauté shallots, ginger, garlic, and chili for about 2 minutes, until just softened and fragrant. Stir in 1 cup (250 mL) water. Add ketjap manis, molasses, 1 tbsp lemon juice, star anise, and black pepper. Reduce heat to medium and simmer for 25–30 minutes, until sauce has reduced and is sticky.

Stir in 1 tsp lemon juice. Taste and adjust seasonings as needed. Remove star anise before serving.

Banana Ice Cream

Sometimes it's nice to end a heavy meal on a lighter note, and this vegan version of ice cream is indeed very light. The cornstarch gives it a custardy mouthfeel, but without some of the heaviness that can accompany a dairy-based dessert. This is loosely inspired by pisang goreng, or Indonesian fried bananas; the rum is there partly for flavor, but mostly to prevent the dessert from hardening too much in the freezer.

½ cup (125 mL) brown sugar

3 tbsp cornstarch

1 lb (454 g) very ripe bananas, mashed

14-oz (398-mL) can coconut milk

14-oz (398-mL) can coconut cream

1 lime, zest and juice

1 tbsp rum

In a saucepan on medium heat, whisk together brown sugar and cornstarch until thoroughly combined. Add bananas, coconut milk, and coconut cream, and bring to a gentle boil, whisking frequently until mixture has thickened.

Remove pan from heat, and whisk in lime zest and juice and rum. Cover with plastic wrap, laying plastic directly on top of mixture to prevent a skin from forming. Refrigerate for at least 4 and up to 48 hours.

Process in an ice cream maker according to manufacturer's instructions, then freeze for at least 4 hours before serving. If it is too firm to scoop right out of the freezer, let it stand for about 10 minutes at room temperature.

Licorice

Dutch candy stores feature row upon row of drop—the Dutch word for licorice—salty or sweet, soft or hard, or some combination of all of these. You make your way down the rows, deciding if you want zoet (sweet) or zoute (salty) or even salmiak (flavored with ammonium chloride), plopping your selection into cone-shaped plastic bags, which fit nicely into your coat pocket. Some licorice is soft and gummy, and some is made of salty powder pressed into tablets, like little pills. Some is made with honig—honey—and used as a tastier version of a cough drop. My favorite kind are the little herring-shaped ones, a little salty and not too hard, somewhere between a wine gum and a lozenge, texture-wise, but infinitely more flavorful.

Licorice (*Glycyrrhiza glabra*) has been used medicinally for thousands of years, from the Mediterranean to China. In moderate amounts, it has some anti-inflammatory properties. Pliny the Elder, in *Naturalis Historia* (c.77 AD), suggested licorice as a cure for asthma as well as for female infertility. In Ayurvedic medicine, licorice is thought to improve digestion and reduce ulcers; it's also considered anti-inflammatory and antimicrobial. However, in my favorite scientific paper of all time, "Licorice Abuse: Time to Send a Warning Message" (online at https://www.ncbi.nlm.nih.gov/pmc/articles/PMC3498851), the nutritional value of licorice "is overrated by many who consume significant amounts and are prone to complications." Eaten to excess, licorice can cause diarrhea, muscle weakness, liver trouble, and hypokalemia, a dangerously low level of potassium in the blood which can be life-threatening in extreme cases. According to the US Food and Drug Administration, "several medical journals have linked black licorice to health problems in people over forty, some of whom had a history of heart disease and/or high blood pressure" (online at https://www.fda.gov/ForConsumers/ConsumerUpdates/ucm277152.htm)." I ate enough licorice in the Netherlands where it was so delicious and fresh, that my teeth were stained gray for a couple of days; fortunately, there were no photos, and I was able to find licorice-flavored toothpaste at the pharmacy to solve all my problems (orally and in life). I did not die, but I am still under forty, so I guess that must be why.

And while licorice has been considered medicinal in the Netherlands since the 13th century, it has been more widely enjoyed as a candy since the 1930s. Today, the Dutch lead the world in annual consumption—about four pounds (two kilograms) per person per year. Whether or not this quantity is dangerous depends on the amount of glycyrrhizin in the licorice preparation; glycyrrhizin is the active ingredient. In Finland, one study found a relationship between high levels of consumption of licorice candy by pregnant women and their children's poor performance in tests of memory and cognition eight years later. However, in Iran, where licorice is used in traditional medicine, a study found that licorice root decreased the frequency and severity of hot flashes in menopausal women. It's hard to know how much glycyrrhizin exists in confectionery licorice; the amount may be negligible, or there might be none at all—many varieties of licorice get their taste from anise extract, which contains no glycyrrhizin and is unrelated to the licorice plant.

Whether it is medicinal or dangerous, licorice occupies a special place in Dutch culture—it is as ubiquitous as peppermint is in North America. Though not a native plant (it grows in warmer, more southern European climates), the Netherlands leads the European Union in licorice production, with more than eighty varieties and €170 million in sales each year.

While for many adults not accustomed to licorice—especially the more aggressive varieties, like dubbel-zoute—the strong taste can be something to work up to, for the people of the Netherlands the taste for salty licorice begins in childhood. Salmiak licorice in particular has a sort of addictive quality, a bracing, numbing effect on the tongue not unlike Szechuan peppercorns, and it's the kind of thing that you eat a whole bunch of before you decide whether or not you like it. It's strange if you're not used to it, but it's worth a try. Look for sugar-coated salmiak, which come in little cubes that look a bit like brown sugar. And although they are Swedish, Ikea sells a variety that I think of as a gateway licorice—a little salty, mostly sweet, and enticing in the way that salted caramel is.

Work your way up to it, and I promise you'll grow to love Dutch licorice. Just be careful, especially if you're over forty—I hear that's when all the trouble starts.

Salted Licorice Ice Cream

When I was a kid, I always thought the best part of tiger-tail ice cream was the licorice part. This is not a traditional Dutch recipe, but it felt like a good place to riff on licorice; the flavor also makes a nice conclusion to a rijsttafel. No one has to know that it's flavored with anise.

4 egg yolks

¾ cup (175 mL) granulated sugar

2 cups (500 mL) whole milk

2 cups (500 mL) heavy cream

1 tsp kosher salt

½ cup (125 mL) fancy molasses

1 tbsp anise extract

¼–½ tsp black gel food coloring (optional)

Add about 2 in (5 cm) water to a medium saucepan, and nestle a sturdy glass bowl inside; if water touches bottom of bowl, pour some out. Remove bowl from pot. Place pot on medium heat.

Put egg yolks and sugar in bowl and set aside.

Fill a second saucepan with milk, cream, salt, and molasses, and whisk to combine. Bring to a gentle simmer on medium heat, then remove from heat and set aside.

Meanwhile, return bowl to first saucepan, and whisk yolks for 6–8 minutes, until pale. Remove bowl from heat.

Whisking constantly, pour a thin stream of milk mixture into egg yolks until eggs are thin enough to pour. Then, pour egg mixture into the milk mixture, whisking constantly.

Pour mixture back into bowl, then whisk in anise extract and food coloring. Cover with plastic wrap, and chill for at least 4 and up to 48 hours.

Churn in an ice cream maker according to manufacturer's instructions. Remove to a sealable container, and store in freezer for up to 1 week.

GEZELLIG (COMFORT FOOD)

GEZELLIG (COMFORT FOOD)

At its most simple—and at its best—gezellig (pronounced "he-sell-igh") is a feeling of goodness, of comfort, and of warmth. It's similar to the Danish concept of hygge, which emphasizes mildness, and coziness, and conviviality—everyone in a good mood with cold gin or warm wine and a good book. Gezellig can be a place, a person, a situation—anything that makes you feel at ease and right with the world. Billboards in Aruba used gezelligheid to sell beer (gezellig can translate to "fun" in the right circumstances), and a cafe in Haarlem used a chalkboard outside to advertise gezellig as part of its ambiance.

While I think that, at times, it is necessary to feel the cold and to confront discomfort in whatever form it takes, it is nice to occasionally retreat into a cozy coffee shop with flattering lighting and a pleasing soundtrack, or to eat cheese toast and soup on the couch or with your elbows on the table. Certain foods just taste better when they are tied to specific experiences, and I am convinced that I enjoy certain meals more when the light inside is yellow and outside is dreary. Gezelligheid is well suited to my west coast lifestyle, where it is often damp and foggy. When it's gross outside, I cannot feel bad about eating too much and then napping. Gezellig!

Tucked into old buildings in cities in the Netherlands you will find cozy pubs, not well-lit and therefore comfortable, with beers from local and Belgian breweries and plates of bitterballen or short menus featuring simple soups and stews. In Leiden, a quiet university town in South Holland, we ate mustard soup with dark rye bread and drank chalices of golden ale while our noses ran and our faces thawed from being out in the cold.

We were starving, having walked for hours that morning around the town to find a statue I wanted to see, and when we found a place that looked okay to bring Hunter into—not too fancy, not clearly meant for adults only—we slumped into a booth and sort of dissolved. They were playing emotive '90s rock, the place looked old but tidy, and anything on the menu would have been good. The soup was warm and creamy, and the bread felt insulating, as if eating it provided protection from the worst that January could offer. We were in fine spirits later when we finally found the monument in question, after a lot more walking (I cannot read a map to save my life).

Yellow-lit pubs and soup with buttered bread and Soul Asylum on tinny speakers and wandering through a quiet town in Europe in January are gezellig. And wherever you are reading this, I hope you are covered in a blanket with the very best slippers on your feet. This chapter is about cozy food—the kind that you tie to a particular person or place or moment. I hope you find your gezellig in here. Start by putting on sweatpants.

Stamppots

"Food I have not, but I know that I must die once. If ye then be helped by my death, beat hands on this body, cut it into pieces, and share it out as far as possible."
—Pieter Adriaansz van der Werff, 1574

The most common question I get asked when I talk about my enthusiasm for Dutch food is "How many recipes can there be for boiled mush?"

To be fair, "boiled mush," or stamppot, is the Netherlands' national dish: according to the blog Stuff Dutch People Like (and my mother-in-law), meal prep begins when you "boil the shit out of" a veggie (that probably includes potatoes), and concludes when you mash it into a palatable mush. Serve sausage on the side, of course, unless you have gone out of your way and made meatballs or, in the culinary tradition of everyone's Dutch grandparents, overcooked a small roast.

There are always mushes, but the one I see most often is boerenkool, a mush of potatoes and kale. My mother-in-law keeps large cans of it in her pantry, and the grandkids often make a main course of it at Sunday dinner. Boiled mush is comfort food, and though it is fun to mock this perhaps old-fashioned use of fresh ingredients, there is little that will make you feel warmer or more sated on some cold November night than a generously buttered bowl of stamppot with rookwurst. And if my husband, his father, and his father's father are any indication, it's a lot easier to never stop talking

if you don't actually have to chew. In this way more than any other, stamppots are quintessentially Dutch.

My favorite variation is hutspot, a mush of carrots, potatoes, and onions that is a lot like the Scottish-inflected mushes I grew up with.

Hutspot, and therefore stamppot, seems to have originated in 1574, during the Siege of Leiden. A pivotal point during the Eighty Years' War—during which the rebellious Dutch rose against occupying Spaniards—it was the second siege in a single year and lasted for six months. Many citizens were left starving and indigent—provisions for the resistance lasted a mere two months. At one point, Pieter Adriaansz van der Werff, the mayor of Leiden, offered his arm as food for the people. No one took him up on it, but a statue in his honor stands in Leiden to this day.

On the night the Spanish withdrew from the city, the Dutch discovered a burble of carrots, potatoes, and onions stewing in the cauldrons the Spanish had left behind (possibly an early or frugal take on olla podrida, a Spanish meat and bean stew, which the Dutch later adapted—olipodrigo is an extravagant Dutch interpretation of the dish, which called for more than a dozen types of meat plus whatever vegetables were in season at the time). In *The Sensible Cook*, the cookbook portion of *The Pleasurable Country Life*, a guide to living well for Dutch aristocrats in the seventeenth century, a recipe for "Spanish Hutspot" calls for mutton or veal, simmered for a long time, and finished with butter, parsley, and a drizzle of raw egg yolk mixed with lemon juice. A variation of the dish calls for beef, fresh ginger, and mace, finished with parsley and butter. When the Dutch celebrate their annual October 3rd Festival to commemorate the end of the Siege of Leiden, they mark the occasion with a heaping helping of hutspot for their hot meal.

Hutspot recipes are widely variable in theory, though the modern interpretation is mostly settled on the dish being a mix of potatoes, carrots, and onions. Traditional recipes might have used parsnips or other root vegetables in place of potatoes, as potatoes weren't widely used in northern Europe until the nineteenth century.

Wherever people need nourishment—physical, spiritual, or otherwise—there are mushes. In Mumbai, pav bhaji is a spicy mash of veggies served on fresh bread rolls that people buy from street vendors; for generations of Scots from Edinburgh to Edmonton, roast beast has always been served with a side of neeps 'n' tatties. Show me a person who says they don't like mashed potatoes, and I'll show you someone who is definitely lying.

And so we come to the truth of Dutch cuisine, however maligned and mushy it might be: the Netherlands has a long and diverse culinary history that evolved to meet Dutch peoples' needs, and the Dutch—like all of us, whether we are farmers or people bound to a desk and a screen for too many hours each day—sometimes need a hot bowl of something simple and nourishing that goes well with too much butter and maybe a fried sausage.

There are no bad cuisines: food is inherently good. Stamppot = comfort food, and comfort food = good food.

Potatoes

Potatoes are not native to Europe; they are an import that the Spanish brought from South America, likely in the sixteenth century. They didn't take hold as a staple of Dutch cuisine until about the eighteenth century; during a period of famine potatoes—aardappel—were an inexpensive food source that could be stored for long periods in a cool environment. By the early nineteenth century, potatoes comprised a significant portion of poorer people's diets—in many cases, people ate potatoes at every meal, mostly boiled. Some think that it was during this period that Dutch cuisine moved from a decadent, adventurous diet during the Golden Age into its more modern iteration, which many Dutch people describe as bland and mushy; two world wars and a Great Depression certainly didn't help revolutionize the national cuisine.

According to the Food and Agriculture Organization of the United Nations, "while potato production is declining in most of Europe, the Dutch still plant almost twenty-five percent of their arable land—some 160,000 hectares—with aardappel, and have achieved world record average yields level of more than forty-five tons per hectare. The potato sector is highly mechanized and draws on a list of some 250 approved varieties" (online at http://www. fao.org/potato-2008/en/world/europe.html).

Potatoes are a versatile ingredient, and one now much beloved by Dutch people; potatoes are the foundation of many a stamppot, served in soups and stews and salads, fried into friet and served with frietsaus (like mayonnaise, but lower in fat) or peanut sauce or curry ketchup or, most simply, mashed with milk and butter. It is in their mashed form that potatoes reach their highest potential.

The potato masher is one of the Dutch kitchen's most fundamental tools, but to really elevate potatoes I recommend using a food mill. Use a buttery yellow variety of potatoes, such as Yukon Gold, but avoid waxy red and white potatoes; starchier potatoes like Russets also work well. If using Yukon Golds, wash and chop the potatoes but don't bother to peel them; if using Russets, rinse and then peel and then rinse again before chopping. Make extra, if you can, and use the leftovers as the foundation of the next day's stamppot.

Luscious Mashed Potatoes

Serve with additional butter once plated because the secret to good mashed potatoes is that they taste like they are mostly butter.

2 lb (900 g) yellow-fleshed potatoes, such as Yukon Gold
1 tbsp kosher salt
½ cup (125 mL) butter
½ cup (125 mL) whole milk
¼ tsp ground nutmeg

In a food mill, cube potatoes, but don't worry about skins; if you don't have a food mill, peel and cube potatoes. Fill a large pot with cold water to cover potatoes by about 1 in (2.5 cm). Add salt. On high heat, bring to a boil and cook until potatoes are tender, 15 to 20 minutes.

Drain potatoes in a colander in the sink. If you have a gas stove, turn heat to low; if you have an electric stove, turn burner off. Return empty pot to stove. Add butter, milk, and nutmeg and let warm together in pot.

Pass potatoes through a food mill directly into pot. If you don't have a food mill, mash thoroughly with a good potato masher. Using a spatula, gently fold milk and butter into potatoes. Taste, adjusting seasonings as needed.

Braised Beef with Sauerkraut Stamppot

Dutch braised beef—called draadjesvlees—fills your home with a rich savoriness long before it even finishes cooking. I buy braising steak when it's on sale at the supermarket, but check with your butcher—if they don't know what you mean by "braising steak," ask for blade steak (in large sections, at least 1 in [2.5 cm] thick) or chuck. A shot of gin in the braising liquid replaces juniper in more traditional recipes; pour a shot for yourself and relax, it'll be a while. Serve with pickles and mustard.

3 tsp kosher salt, divided

3 lb (1.3 kg) blade steak or
    braising roast

4 slices bacon, cut into lardons

1 onion, diced

3 garlic cloves, roughly chopped

2 tbsp gin

1 tbsp all-purpose flour

1 tsp ground black pepper,
    divided

¼ tsp ground nutmeg

2 fresh thyme sprigs

2 bay leaves

2 cups (500 mL) chicken stock

2 lb (900 g) potatoes, peeled
    and diced

1 14-oz (398-mL) jar
    sauerkraut

4 tbsp butter, divided

½ cup (125 mL) whole milk

2 cups (500 mL) mushrooms,
    sliced

2 tsp minced fresh thyme leaves

3 green onions, finely chopped

Sprinkle 1 tsp kosher salt on each side of steak, massaging it into meat. Set aside.

Preheat oven to 325°F (165°C).

In a Dutch oven on medium-high heat, cook bacon for about 6 minutes, until crisp. Remove bacon to a plate lined with paper towels and set aside.

Using tongs, place meat in pot to sear. If too big, cut it in half. Cook each side for about 3 minutes, until deeply browned. Remove browned meat to a plate and set aside.

Add onions and garlic. Stir in gin, scraping browned bits off bottom of pot. Sauté for about 3 minutes, until onions are translucent. Stir in flour, 1 tsp salt, ½ tsp pepper, and nutmeg, and stir to coat.

Place thyme sprigs and bay leaves in pot. Return beef to pot. Add chicken stock, then top up with water as needed so that liquid covers beef halfway. Bring liquid to a boil, cover pot with lid and bake for 2½ hours.

In the last 30 minutes, add potatoes to a large pot of water with remainder of salt. On high, bring to a boil and cook for about 15 minutes, until potatoes are easily pierced with the tip of a sharp knife. Add sauerkraut, cook for 3 minutes, then drain. Reduce heat to medium, then return pot to stove.

Add 2 tbsp butter and all the milk. Return potatoes and sauerkraut to pot. Add reserved bacon, and mash to desired consistency, adding more milk if needed.

Meanwhile, in a frying pan on medium-high heat, melt 2 tbsp butter. Add sliced mushrooms and sauté, stirring frequently for about 6 minutes, until mushrooms are just browned.

Remove meat from oven. Using tongs, gently lift meat out of braising liquid. Remove bay leaves and thyme sprigs and discard.

Place pot on medium-high heat. Pour browned mushrooms with thyme leaves into pot, and stir for about 5 minutes, until liquid has reduced slightly.

Spoon sauerkraut stamppot mixture onto a large serving platter. Sprinkle with minced green onions. Place braised beef on top of stamppot. Serve with mushroom gravy, either poured over top or on the side.

Basic Hutspot

For this recipe, or any recipe involving mashed starchy vegetables, I recommend using a food mill to achieve the best possible texture. Serve with sausage or roast meat.

2 lb (900 g) Russet or other starch potato, peeled and cubed

2 lb carrots (900 g) peeled and chopped, divided

1 lb (454 g) onions, diced

2 garlic cloves

1 bay leaf

1 tbsp kosher salt

¼ cup butter, melted

¼ tsp ground nutmeg

salt, to taste

Place potatoes, 1 lb carrots, onions, garlic, and bay leaf in a large pot. Add salt, then fill with cold water to cover. On medium-high heat, bring to a boil, then reduce heat, and simmer for about 15 minutes, until potatoes are tender.

Meanwhile, add remainder of carrots and 1 tsp salt to a small pot. Fill with cold water to cover. On medium-high heat, bring to a boil, and cook for about 10 minutes or until tender. Drain carrots, then mash and set aside.

Drain potato mixture, and discard bay leaf. Pass potato mixture through a food mill set to medium. Some liquid will come out of carrots and onions; drain off as needed.

Stir butter and nutmeg in to puréed potato mixture. Taste and adjust seasoning as needed. Fold in mashed carrots. Serve hot.

Hachee with Beer & Apples

One of my prerequisites for comfort food is that it must be paired with a starchy buttered carbohydrate, ideally bread or potatoes. This one goes with both, and it's brown. Brown foods with white carbs are understood by all cultures to be perfect foods—it is, perhaps, the one thing we can all agree on. Bring people together with this soothing beef stew.

4 slices bacon or salt pork, finely chopped

2 lb (900 g) beef chuck, cubed

1 tbsp butter

2 lb (900 g) onions, halved lengthwise and thinly sliced

2 garlic cloves, smashed

3 tbsp all-purpose flour

2 tbsp molasses

2 tsp kosher salt

1 tsp ground black pepper

½ tsp ground nutmeg

1 bay leaf

12 oz (355 mL) amber or brown ale (nothing hoppy)

2 lb (900 g) firm-fleshed apples, peeled, cored, and cut into wedges approximately ½-in (1-cm) thick

4 cups low-sodium or homemade chicken stock

2 tsp apple cider vinegar

salt, to taste

2 tbsp chopped fresh parsley, for garnish

In a Dutch oven or other heavy pot on medium-high heat, fry bacon, stirring frequently, for about 4 minutes, until fat has rendered out and bacon is crispy. Remove bacon to a plate lined with paper towels, and set aside.

Working in batches, brown beef in bacon fat. As beef browns, remove from pot and set aside.

Add butter to pot and let melt. Stir in onions. Reduce heat to medium. Brown onions for about 15–20 minutes, stirring frequently, until mostly caramelized and reduced in volume by about two-thirds.

Add garlic. Return beef and bacon to pot. Add flour, and stir to coat thoroughly. Add molasses, salt, pepper, and nutmeg, and stir again. Add bay leaf.

Add beer to pot, scraping up any browned bits. The brown bits make this stew what it is. Add apples and chicken stock.

Reduce heat to medium-low, and simmer, uncovered, for 2½–3 hours, until sauce has thickened and meat is tender.

Before serving, stir in apple cider vinegar. Taste and adjust seasoning as needed. Sprinkle parsley over finished dish and serve.

Farmer's Cheese Soup

Serve this soup the way you would serve French onion soup—in oven-safe dishes so you can broil the bread and cheese in the serving bowl. If you don't have oven-safe serving ware, broil the bread and cheese separately, then add them to the soup before serving.

2 slices bacon, chopped

1 onion, diced

2 garlic cloves, minced

2 tsp kosher salt

2 lb (900 g) cauliflower, trimmed and chopped

1 lb (454 g) yellow-fleshed potatoes, such as Yukon Gold, peeled and diced

4 cups (1 L) homemade or low-sodium chicken stock

2 cups (500 mL) whole milk

3 tbsp butter

6 slices rye bread, trimmed to fit serving bowls

½ cup (125 mL) finely shredded aged Gouda or Parmesan cheese

½ cup (125 mL) cream

½ tsp ground black pepper

½ tsp ground nutmeg

4 tsp minced fresh thyme

1 cup (250 mL) shredded smoked Gouda

In a frying pan on medium heat, fry bacon for about 3 minutes, until it begins to brown a little and release fat.

Stir in onions and garlic and sauté for 3–4 minutes, until onions begin to sweat. Add salt, cauliflower, potatoes, stock, and milk and bring to a simmer. Simmer for 15–20 minutes, until cauliflower and potatoes are tender.

Preheat broiler.

Spread ½ tbsp butter on each piece of bread. Lay sliced bread, butter-side up, on a baking sheet. Broil for about 6 minutes (but start checking after about 3 minutes), until toasted and crisp.

Stir cheese into soup. Using either an immersion or stand blender, purée until smooth. Use caution when working around hot liquids. If using a stand blender, work in batches; do not fill more than halfway.

Return soup to stove, then whisk in cream, pepper, and nutmeg. Adjust seasonings to taste.

Ladle soup into bowls, and top each bowl with a piece of toasted bread. Sprinkle ½ tsp fresh thyme on each, then about 2 tbsp shredded cheese.

Place under broiler and broil for about 5 minutes (begin checking after about 3 minutes), until cheese is bubbly and golden in places.

Farmer's Cheese Soup cont'd

If you don't have oven-safe bowls, prepare toasts ahead of time by sprinkling thyme and cheese on toasted bread slices and broiling for 3–5 minutes. Gently transfer toasts to soup in bowls, and serve immediately.

Mustard Soup

Your guests may not detect the mustard at first taste. This mosterdsoep (mustard soup) has the effect of being familiar without knocking you over the head about it—it's the kind of thing that tastes perfect after a chilly fall day or an afternoon building snowmen in the park. I enjoy mine with a heel of crusty bread (or a Cheese Toastie, p. 109) while wearing the fluffiest socks I can find.

2 slices bacon, sliced into lardons

2 cups (500 mL) thinly sliced leeks, white and light green parts only

½ lb (250 g) starchy potatoes, such as Russets, peeled and diced

1 garlic clove, smashed

4 cups (4 L) chicken stock

1 tsp kosher salt

½ cup (125 mL) sour cream + more for garnish

2 tbsp grainy Dijon mustard

4 egg yolks

½ tsp yellow curry powder

salt, to taste

Maggi seasoning, for garnish

¼ cup (60 mL) chopped fresh chives or green onions, for garnish

In a Dutch oven or other heavy pot on medium-high heat, fry bacon for about 4 minutes, until crispy. Remove and set aside on a plate lined with paper towels. Pour off all but 2 tbsp fat; if more is needed, add butter.

Add leeks and quickly stir to coat in fat. Add potatoes and garlic. Stir in chicken stock, scraping up any browned bits. Add salt, and bring liquid to a boil. Reduce heat to medium, and simmer for about 10 minutes, until potatoes are tender.

Meanwhile, in a bowl, whisk together sour cream, mustard, egg yolks, curry powder, and 2 tbsp cold water, and set aside.

Remove pot from heat and purée with immersion or stand blender. If using a stand blender, first let cool for about 10 minutes. Use caution when working with hot liquids. Working in batches, fill blender only half way, then purée until smooth. Return mixture to medium heat and bring back to a boil.

Remove mixture from heat, and, working quickly, pour sour cream mixture into soup in a thin stream while whisking constantly. Don't let eggs become scrambled. Taste and adjust seasonings as needed.

Serve topped with reserved bacon, a dollop of additional sour cream, Maggi (if you've got it), and chopped fresh chives.

Maggi Meatball Soup

The most common disagreement I have with Nick is over whether it is appropriate to splash a tablespoon of Maggi into dinner before even tasting it, fundamentally altering the flavor of something I have lovingly prepared. Against all odds, we are somehow still together. This soup is a compromise, a bit like his mother's version, with meatballs flavored with Maggi seasoning. Like my mother-in-law, you could serve this for lunch on Sunday with soft, buttered buns and thin slices of deli ham and Gouda.

MEATBALLS

½ lb (454 g) extra lean ground beef

½ cup (125 mL) bread crumbs

1 egg

1 tbsp Maggi

½ tsp ground nutmeg

½ tsp ground black pepper

1 garlic clove, finely chopped

SOUP

2 tbsp olive oil

2 carrots, quartered lengthwise and chopped

2 celery stalks, quartered lengthwise and chopped

1 shallot, chopped

1 garlic clove, minced

2 tsp kosher salt

2 tsp yellow curry powder

1 bay leaf

6 cups (1.5 L) low-sodium or homemade chicken stock

½ cup (125 mL) fine egg noodles

salt, to taste

1 tbsp fresh lemon juice

½ cup (125mL) roughly chopped fresh parsley leaves

In a large bowl, combine ground beef, bread crumbs, egg, Maggi, nutmeg, pepper, and garlic with your hands, until well mixed. Form into meatballs about ½-in (1-cm) in diameter (about 40). Set aside.

In a large pot on medium-high heat, add oil, carrots, celery, shallots, and garlic, and sauté for about 2 minutes, until colors have brightened and everything's coated in oil. Add salt, curry powder, and bay leaf, and cook for another 1–2 minutes, until curry is fragrant and starting to stick to bottom of pot. Stir in stock.

Bring soup to a boil, then reduce heat to medium. Drop meatballs into pot, stirring gently, and let simmer for 10 minutes.

Add egg noodles and cook for another 5 minutes, until noodles are al dente.

Adjust seasoning to taste. Stir in lemon juice and parsley and remove bay leaf.

Snert
(Dutch Split-Pea Soup)

You don't just make a little snert. And that's a good thing, because you don't just want a little snert—you want enough to warm the chill in your cheeks after an afternoon outside in the bracing cold. You want to have another bowl, maybe, and a lot of buttered rye bread, a strong Belgian beer, and a little bowl of pickled onions on the side. If you've made more than you can eat, new moms everywhere would love for you to drop off a container.

1–2 lb (454–900 g) whole pork butt or shoulder

4 slices bacon, sliced into lardons

1 onion, diced

1 lb (454 g) carrots, peeled and diced

1 lb (454 g) celeriac, peeled and diced

½ lb (250 g) starchy potatoes, such as Russet, peeled and diced

4 garlic cloves, minced

2 bay leaves

2 tsp kosher salt

2 tsp ground cumin

1 tsp smoked paprika

1 tsp dried thyme

½ tsp ground black pepper

2 cups (500 mL) split green peas, rinsed

1 lb (454 g) smoked pork sausage, cut into bite-sized pieces

salt, to taste

1 tsp grainy Dijon mustard

4 green onions, finely chopped

Place pork butt in a large pot, and cover completely with cold water. Bring to a boil on high heat, and boil for 10 minutes.

Remove pork butt and set aside. Drain and wipe pot to remove scum.

Return pot to stove on medium-high heat. Add bacon and fry for 3–5 minutes, until fat has rendered and bacon is very crisp but not burnt. Drain off all but 3 tbsp fat.

Add onions, carrots, celeriac, and potatoes, stirring to coat in fat. Add garlic, bay leaves, salt, cumin, paprika, thyme, and pepper. Stir again to coat vegetables in spice mixture.

Add split peas, and stir to combine. Make a well in middle of peas, and nestle pork butt into well.

Pour 12 cups (about 3 L) cold water into pot and increase heat to high. Bring liquid up to a gentle boil, then reduce heat to medium-low and simmer for 2½–3 hours, until peas have dissolved and vegetables have begun to disintegrate. If soup begins to boil, reduce heat; it should not exceed a simmer.

 Remove pork from pot to a cutting board and let cool. Add sausages to soup and continue to simmer on low heat.

Snert (Dutch Split-Pea Soup) cont'd

Using 2 forks—and being careful not to burn your fingers—
shred pork, removing large hunks of fat that haven't broken
down during cooking. Return pork to pot, and stir to combine.
Taste and adjust seasoning as needed.

Before serving, stir in grainy Dijon mustard and fresh green
onions.

Kale & Potato Soup

I like kale—but not everyone does. Some of those kale opponents might be loitering in your kitchen right now, complaining because they are ungrateful. Trick them with this very simple but totally unusual soup, which combines pedestrian ingredients like kale and potatoes with fresh dill and buttermilk for a tart, pickle-ish soup that they won't even realize is good for them.

2 tbsp butter

1 large onion, diced

2 garlic cloves

2 lb (900 g) yellow-fleshed potatoes, such as Yukon Gold, peeled and cubed

2 tsp kosher salt

½ tsp ground black pepper

½ tsp ground nutmeg

4 cups (1 L) low-sodium or homemade chicken stock

1 lb (454 g) curly kale, rinsed, stems removed

½ cup (125 mL) packed fresh dill

1½ cups (375 mL) buttermilk

salt and pepper, to taste

In a Dutch oven on medium-high heat, melt butter. Add onions and sauté for about 5 minutes, until golden. Add garlic, stirring to coat in butter, then add cubed potatoes. Add salt, pepper, and nutmeg. Stir to coat vegetables in spices.

Add chicken stock. Bring up to a simmer, then reduce heat to medium. Simmer for 15 minutes, or until potatoes are tender.

Chop kale roughly and add to soup. Cook for about 3 minutes, until kale has wilted but retains bright color. Add dill.

Purée with an immersion blender. Or use a stand blender, working in batches. Use care around hot liquids, and fill blender only half full. Pulse gently at first.

Return soup to pot and bring back to a simmer. Gently stir in buttermilk. Taste, adjusting seasonings as needed. Thin to desired consistency with additional stock or water.

Brown Beans & Pork

A sweet, savory stew of tender pork and beans cooked low and slow will soothe you no matter what time of year it is, though this dish is perfect for when it's sweater weather and you have nothing to do all afternoon but read a new book. Typically, this dish might use a variety of brown beans widely available in the Netherlands; I find canned or pre-cooked pinto beans work just fine. It's also great the next day, so if you made it on Sunday, you could look forward to it all day on Monday. Serve with buttered bread and cold applesauce.

2 tbsp canola or vegetable oil, divided

1 lb (454 g) pork butt or shoulder, cubed

1 tbsp butter

1 lb (454 g) onions, finely chopped

½ lb (225 g) apples, peeled and diced

1 garlic clove, minced

2 tbsp tomato paste

2 tsp kosher salt

2 tsp smoked paprika

½ tsp ground black pepper

¼ tsp ground cinnamon

1 bay leaf

1 cup (250 mL) apple cider or unsweetened apple juice

1 tbsp brown sugar

¼ cup (60 mL) molasses

12 oz (355 mL) dark beer

2 19-oz (540-mL) cans pinto beans, drained and rinsed

2 tsp apple cider vinegar

salt and pepper, to taste

In a Dutch oven on medium-high, heat oil. Brown cubed pork, about 3 minutes per side, then remove to a bowl and set aside.

Add butter to pot, and reduce heat to medium. Add onions and sauté, stirring regularly, for about 15 minutes, until golden and just starting to brown. Add apples and garlic and sauté for 2–3 minutes, until apples have begun to release moisture.

Add tomato paste, salt, paprika, pepper, and cinnamon, and cook for about 4 minutes, until liquid has evaporated and tomato paste has begun to brown and stick.

Add bay leaf and apple cider. Scrape bottom of pot to incorporate tomato paste. Stir in brown sugar and molasses. Increase heat and bring to a simmer. Add beer, then bring back up to a simmer.

Cover, and reduce heat to low. Cook for 2 hours, stirring periodically.

Remove cover. Add beans, partially cover, and cook for about 10 more minutes, until sauce has thickened and reduced slightly and beans have softened a bit. Stir in apple cider vinegar. Adjust seasonings to taste.

Serve hot, in bowls.

Beef Pastechi

We bought these on a whim in Aruba, thinking we'd eat one in the rental car on the way to our destination—The Donkey Sanctuary in Santa Cruz—and then grab lunch, but instead we ate a whole bag of them and had zero regrets. They are sweet and savory at the same time, and somewhere between chewy and crispy, so they don't crumble in your hands as you shove them into your face, one after the other.

2 tbsp butter

1 onion, finely chopped

1 celery stalk, finely chopped

1 red bell pepper, finely
    chopped

2 garlic cloves, minced

1 lb (454 g) lean ground beef

2 tbsp tomato paste

2 tbsp + 1 ¼ cups (310 mL) all-
    purpose flour, divided

¼ cup (60 mL) soy sauce

2 tsp yellow curry powder

1 tsp ground cumin

1 lime, zest and juice

½ tsp ground black pepper

½ cup (125 mL) milk

2 tbsp granulated sugar

½ cup (125 mL) semolina flour

2 tbsp butter

½ tsp salt

¼ tsp nutmeg

4–6 cups (1–1.5 L) vegetable or
    canola oil, for frying

In a frying pan on medium-high heat, melt butter and sauté onions, celery, and bell peppers for about 3 minutes, until they've brightened in color and begun to sweat.

Add garlic and sauté for another minute, and then crumble ground beef into pan and cook for about 4 minutes, until beef is mostly cooked through.

Add tomato paste and 2 tbsp flour, and mix to combine well.

Add soy sauce, curry powder, cumin, lime zest and juice, and pepper, and simmer for about 3 minutes, until liquid has mostly evaporated. Remove from heat and allow to cool completely.

Meanwhile, in a pot on medium-high heat, bring 1 cup (250 mL) water, milk, and sugar to a boil. Whisk in semolina and cook for 1–2 minutes, until thickened. Add butter, salt and nutmeg, then remove from heat.

Gently fold 1 cup (250 mL) flour into semolina mixture until a dough forms. Cover and let rest 10 minutes, or until cool enough to handle.

Knead dough for about 3 minutes, adding remainder of flour 1 tbsp at a time as needed, until no longer sticky.

Divide dough into 8 equal pieces. Roll into circles about 5–6 in (15–20-cm) in diameter, and ¼-in (6-mm) thick. Place

Beef Pastechi cont'd

2–3 tbsp filling in each. Fold dough over filling. Press edges of dough together gently, then seal by pressing down around edges with the tines of a fork.

In a Dutch oven or other sturdy pot on medium-high, heat oil to about 350°F (175°C). Working in batches, deep-fry, flipping once to cook both sides, until crisp and golden, about 2 minutes per side. Drain on a plate lined with paper towels and serve hot.

Cranberry & Persimmon Pastechi

MAKES 8

Pastechi are an empanada-like treat made in the Dutch Caribbean. This sweet version with cranberries and persimmon is maybe not traditional, but it is a great way to use what's in season during the fall. In the Netherlands, persimmons are often called Kaki or Sharon fruit, and are available in late fall and early winter.

1 lb (454 g) Fuyu persimmons, trimmed and diced

2 cups (500 mL) fresh or frozen cranberries

½ cup (125 mL) + 3 tbsp granulated sugar, divided

½ cup (125 mL) whole milk

½ cup (125 mL) semolina flour

2 tbsp butter

½ tsp kosher salt

¼ tsp ground nutmeg

1¼ cups (310 mL) all-purpose flour, divided

4–6 cups (1–1.5 L) vegetable or canola oil, for frying

In a small saucepan on medium-high heat, cook persimmons and cranberries with ½ cup (125 mL) sugar for 10–12 minutes, stirring frequently, until cranberries have burst and mixture has become jammy. Set aside to cool.

Meanwhile, in pot on medium-high heat, add 1 cup (250 mL) water, milk, and 3 tbsp sugar, and bring to a boil. Whisk in semolina and cook for 1–2 minutes, until thickened. Add butter, salt and nutmeg, then remove from heat.

Gently fold 1 cup (250 mL) flour into semolina mixture until a dough forms. Cover and let rest for 10 minutes, or until cool enough to handle. Use remainder of flour (1 tbsp at a time, as needed) to knead dough for about 3 minutes, or until it's no longer sticky.

Divide dough into 8 equal pieces. Roll into circles about 5–6 in (12–15 cm) in diameter, ¼ in (6 mm) thick. Place 2–3 tbsp filling in each, folding dough over filling. Press dough together gently, then seal by pressing down around edges with tines of a fork.

In a Dutch oven or other heavy pot, heat oil to about 350°F (175°C). Working in batches, deep-fry, about 2 minutes per side, until crisp and golden.

Drain on a plate lined with paper towels, sprinkle with remaining sugar, and serve hot.

Hunter's Chocolate Peanut Butter Pitcher Pudding

The dairy section in most Dutch grocery stores is expansive, and the highlight for my son Hunter was the milk cartons full of cold pudding—called vla—in all kinds of flavors (and several chocolate varieties). The Netherlands is his spiritual homeland, and innumerable pudding varieties may be the main reason. This recipe makes a pudding of about the same consistency, in his preferred flavor, which we keep in a pitcher in the fridge just for him.

½ cup (125 mL) granulated sugar

½ cup (125 mL) brown sugar

5 tbsp Dutch process cocoa powder

2 tbsp cornstarch

3 cups (750 mL) whole milk

2 tbsp creamy peanut butter

¼ tsp kosher salt

1 tsp vanilla extract

½ cup (125 mL) heavy cream

In a saucepan on medium-high heat, whisk together sugars, cocoa, and cornstarch. Gradually add milk, whisking to prevent clumps from forming. Add peanut butter and salt, and whisk until mixture is smooth.

Bring to a boil, and then, still whisking briskly, cook for 1–2 minutes to thicken. Remove from heat. Stir in vanilla extract and cream.

Pour into a pitcher or 1-qt (1-L) Mason jar to cool, whisking occasionally as it cools to prevent a skin from forming. Refrigerate, and serve cold after dinner.

Semolina Pudding with Rose & Honey

This is a not-too-sweet dessert, a gentle finish to brunch or a soothing weeknight nightcap. The rose flavor is not intense, but just enough to transport you, even for a moment, to the Dutch countryside in spring. This pudding doesn't keep well in the refrigerator—it will turn rubbery once it's cold and set—so plan to eat it right away. Serve with a dollop of whipped cream and toasted pistachios or with a spoonful of raspberry jam.

2 egg yolks, beaten
½ cup (125 mL) heavy cream
2 cups (500 mL) whole milk
¼ cup (60 mL) honey
1½ tsp rose water
½ cup (125 mL) semolina
1 tbsp butter

In a bowl, combine beaten egg yolks and heavy cream. Set aside.

In a saucepan on medium-high heat, whisk together whole milk, honey, and rose water. Bring just to a boil, then gradually add semolina. It will thicken almost immediately.

Remove pot from heat, and gently pour a stream of semolina mixture into egg yolk mixture, whisking continuously. Return to heat, and still whisking constantly, cook for 30–60 seconds, until mixture is thick and eggs cooked through. Whisk in butter.

Divide mixture evenly between four to six 6-oz (175-mL) ramekins. Let stand for 15 minutes. Serve warm.

Chipolata Pudding (Dutch Trifle)

Fair warning—this one's on the boozy side. Does it need all that rum? Maybe not, but I stand by the recipe in all its alcoholic glory. I like to serve this to friends to finish a Saturday lunch, because it's best made a day or two ahead, and because, like trifle, it's delicious but kind of a mess.

Tip: The recipe is easily halved; use the same amount of orange juice but half the zest.

11 oz (300 g) store-bought ladyfinger cookies

½ cup (125 mL) apricot jam

1 large navel orange, juice and zest

12 egg yolks

1 ½ cups (375 mL) + 2 tbsp granulated sugar, divided

¾ cup (175 mL) amber or dark rum

pinch salt

2 tsp vanilla extract, divided

1 cup (250 mL) whipping cream

Line an 8-cup (2-L) trifle bowl with ladyfingers, crumbling any that don't fit and pressing crumbled bits between gaps. Alternatively, divide cookies between ten 6-oz (175-mL) ramekins or 1-cup (250-mL) mason jars.

In a small bowl, combine jam and orange juice. In a microwave or small saucepan on medium heat, warm jam mixture for 2 minutes, until thinned. Stir in zest. Pour mixture evenly over ladyfingers.

In a small saucepan on medium, heat about 1 in (2.5 cm) water to a simmer. In a large glass bowl that will nestle into saucepan without touching water, whisk egg yolks with 1½ cups (175 mL) sugar for about 4 minutes, until sugar has mostly dissolved. Add rum, whisk to combine, then place bowl into pot of water on stove.

Whisk mixture constantly for about 10 minutes, until custard has thickened. To test, dip the back of a spoon into mixture and run a finger down the middle—if custard doesn't run to fill gap, it's cooked. Remove custard from heat. Stir in 1 tsp vanilla extract.

Pour custard over ladyfingers, and cover with plastic wrap, making a seal to prevent custard from forming a skin. Refrigerate for at least 12 hours or up to 3 days.

Before serving: In a bowl, using a stand mixer, hand-held mixer, or whisk, whip cream to desired consistency with 2 tbsp sugar and 1 tsp vanilla extract, then dollop over top, spreading to evenly cover custard.

Chocolate

I think the moment Hunter felt most at home in the Netherlands is when Nick dragged us all into a brewery. We sat down at a table—there were no other kids around—and Nick opened the menu and there it was, not on a kids' menu, but on the regular, grown-ass adult menu: a chocolate sandwich. "I can have a chocolate sandwich?!" Hunter was incredulous.

Chocolate is big in the Netherlands, and it is everywhere from sandwich sprinkles and spreads to pudding to drinking chocolate—warme chocolademelk—and mocha cakes. At Christmas, children receive chocolate letters. Historically, these were so that each child would know which pile of treats belonged to her, but today they are most often placed in a shoe during Sinterklaas, the same way many families in North America would fill a child's stocking on Christmas Eve.

Chocolate became popular with—and accessible to—Dutch consumers in the nineteenth century after a series of innovations made it possible to produce with a reliable standard of quality. Chocolate is naturally acidic, and "Dutch process" cocoa is alkalized to balance the taste and reduce some of the bitterness associated with natural cocoa. Prior to the discovery of this process (by Dutch chocolatier Coenraad Johannes van Houten), chocolate was mainly served as a drink. Now it could be used in cakes, cookies, and confectionery; Dutch process cocoa is often used in baking where baking powder is used as the leavener.

The Netherlands imports more cocoa beans per year than anywhere else in the world and has a huge cocoa-processing industry, the second largest in the world. On average, the Dutch consume just over ten pounds (4.5 kg) of chocolate per person per year, more than Americans but significantly less than some of their European neighbors. This is perhaps because chocolate is considered more of a flavoring than a snack—cocoa powder is used in dairy-based drinks and desserts, mixed with other ingredients to form spreads and sauces, and you can order an elegant, delicious hot chocolate made with as much care and attention as an espresso in any café. In addition, over the past decade Dutch people have been mindful about how their chocolate is produced, and have demonstrated a preference for higher-end, better quality, Fair Trade or other certified products. Many Dutch people will choose a small amount of costlier, higher-quality chocolate, but less frequently. Chocolate is big, but it's also a big treat.

In my opinion, the best way to enjoy chocolate in the Netherlands is in the form that the Dutch do best: gently sweetened, warmed with good quality milk, and topped with as much whipped cream as your mug can manage.

Hot Chocolate

Where we live, it rains a lot—all the time for some parts of the year—and so we make the best of it. Hunter watches for puddles forming on the sidewalk, and when they are deep enough, he grabs his rubber boots and raincoat and demands to go outside. Aside from puddle-jumping, one of Hunter's great joys is, after playing in the rain, warming up with a mug of hot chocolate—there's not really any other time when he asks for it, so I am fairly certain he has tied a mug of chocolate and whipped cream to a feeling. Puddles are gezellig. Hot chocolate is gezellig. Of course, whipped cream is gezellig. Fair warning: This is pretty rich stuff. If serving to grownups, you can thin it out with a bit of rum or Kahlua.

Tip: You can make the hot chocolate ahead of time and reheat it—just rewarm gently on medium heat. It will last for 3 days in a sealed jar in the fridge; shake before pouring the liquid back in the pot.

2 tbsp butter

2 tbsp Dutch process cocoa
   powder

¼ cup (60mL) granulated sugar

2.5 cups (625 mL) whole milk

½ cup (125mL) heavy cream

1 cup (250mL) semisweet
   chocolate chips

1 tsp vanilla extract

In a heavy-bottomed saucepan on medium heat, melt butter. Whisk in cocoa powder and sugar, then pour in milk and cream. Cook, whisking constantly, about 1 minute, until mixture feels lukewarm to the touch, then add chocolate chips.

Whisk constantly for 10–15 minutes, until it just comes to a boil. Whisk in vanilla.

Divide between six mugs and serve.

CHRISTMAS

CHRISTMAS

The Christmas season in the Netherlands begins with the arrival of Sinterklaas on December 5, followed by the feast of Saint Nicholas on December 6. Christmas is also celebrated over two days, with First and Second Christmas Day falling on December 25 and 26. This is very civilized, I think, especially if you are espoused and have two sets of parents to visit. When one might exchange gifts, if at all, is largely dependent on your own family traditions—some celebrate with gifts on the 5th or the 6th, while others wait until Christmas Eve or Christmas morning. Some households don't do gifts at all. And while Sinterklaas has reigned as the supreme Christmas character for hundreds of years, Santa Claus has been horning his way into the Dutch market—he is called de Kerstman there.

But Christmas in the Netherlands is not generally accompanied by the garish commercialism of a North American Christmas; it's there, of course, but to a much smaller degree. December in the Netherlands is a time to cuddle up, settle in, and feast with your favorite friends and family, and to revel in all of the best parts of the season. Every town and village decorates for the season, with twinkling lights strung across the lanes and decorated trees in town squares, and most cities and towns have Christmas markets with—in some cases—hundreds of stalls selling treats like fresh pretzels and poffertjes (p. 218), warm Bishop's wine (p. 232), and attractions including carnival rides, petting zoos, or skating. Christmas markets are a celebration of Dutch culture.

If you think the Dutch don't have a sense of humor, then you probably just aren't in on the joke.

The festive season is both secular and religious. The traditional religions of the Netherlands are primarily based in Christianity, with Catholicism in the south and Calvinism (a form of Protestantism) in the north. A primary impetus for the Eighty Years' War, which began in 1566, was rebellion among Dutch Calvinists against the Spanish (Catholic) occupiers in response to religious persecution under the Spanish Inquisition. The Netherlands, as a result, has a legacy of religious tolerance, for the most part.

Currently, nearly seventy percent of the population of the Netherlands is secular, with no religious affiliation; most self-identify as agnostic or "spiritual but not religious." However, it is traditional to attend Christmas Eve services.

Christmas Day (and Second Christmas Day) are all about food. Traditionally, game meats like rabbit and venison have been popular. Elegantly prepared pork—rollade—or beef roast are also acceptable. Turkey is not popular, though it is growing in popularity, possibly due to the influence of a large North American immigrant community. Many families enjoy gourmetten, a style of feast in which individuals cook small morsels of meat and vegetables on a communal griddle, melting cheese on paddles beneath the griddle to pour on top. On the side, a simple lettuce salad (p. 213) and pickles of all sorts cut the richness of the meats and cheeses. We did this with Nick's family a few years ago, and it went well until everyone hit their cheese-breaking point and sort of slumped over and couldn't speak for a long time. We haven't done it since. There's no real recipe for gourmetten—it's mostly a mix of bits of steak, thin slices of bacon, rounds of sausage, and veggies like mushrooms topped with cheese, but if you're interested in hosting your own gourmetten, look for cooking surfaces called "party grills" or "raclette" by brands like Swissmar. Nick is deeply passionate about melting cheese (I do not understand how he remains thin while I melt considerably less cheese and do not), and so my parents bought him the fancy granite version for his birthday one year and it works very well. Party grills or raclettes cost between $60 and around $200 USD.

Whether you make your celebration simple or elaborate, the most important thing is that you feel snuggly and warm and at peace. Gather your best people and share a table and a lot of Bishop's wine and gin or genever and all your funniest stories (if you think the Dutch don't have a sense of humor, then you probably just aren't in on the joke). Zalig Kerstfeest!

Stuffed Pork Loin

· MAKES 8–10 SERVINGS ·

Beautiful and fragrant, this holiday main is impressive. There's also not much to it, and you can prepare it ahead of time and chill it in the refrigerator for up to two days before cooking. The rolling part is a two-person job—if you have tiny hands, bring in reinforcements. Ask your butcher to butterfly a pork loin, as that's the hardest part. Serve with Roasted Baby Potatoes (p. 209) and Beet & Apple Salad (p. 214).

2 tbsp fennel seeds

2 tbsp butter

1 onion, finely chopped

1 garlic clove, minced

2 Anjou or Bartlett pears, cored and finely chopped

1 cup (250 mL) currants

½ cup (125 mL) bread crumbs

2 tsp + 1 tbsp kosher salt, divided

4–4½-lb (2-kg) pork loin, butterflied

3 tbsp grainy Dijon mustard

1 tbsp minced fresh rosemary

1 tsp ground black pepper

1 cup (250 mL) white wine

1 tbsp olive oil

Preheat oven to 325°F (160°).

In a large frying pan on medium-high heat, toast fennel seeds, shaking pan to move seeds around, for about 2 minutes, until golden. Scrape into a bowl and set aside.

Add butter to pan. Stir in onions. Sauté for about 10 minutes, until onions are soft and golden. Add garlic and cook for 2 minutes.

Transfer onions and garlic to a large bowl. Add pears, currants, bread crumbs, and 1 tsp salt. Gently stir to combine and coat in crumbs. Set aside.

Spread pork loin out so that it sits flat with the fat on the outside, and turn it so that you roll it up with, not against, the grain. (When you slice the cooked loin, you will be slicing against the grain.)

Smear mustard over pork loin, then sprinkle evenly with rosemary, pepper, and 1 tsp salt.

Spoon pear mixture over loin, pressing mixture with your hands to pack it on. (Now, go wash your hands.)

Roll carefully but firmly, so that meat is tight but filling doesn't squish out the sides. CONTINUED ON P.208

Stuffed Pork Loin cont'd

Tie loin every inch (2.5 cm) with butcher's twine or other kitchen string, keeping each loop very tight. (No one wants floppy meat.)

If making this ahead, tightly wrap meat in plastic wrap and refrigerate until ready to roast it. Before roasting, bring the meat back up to room temperature. Prepare as follows, then let it rest for 1 hour in roasting pan at room temperature.

Turn rolled loin seam-side down, and rub with olive oil. Coat with toasted fennel seeds and 1 tbsp salt. Place in roasting pan, then add wine.

Roast on middle rack of oven, turning pan midway through cooking to ensure even browning. Roast for about 75 minutes, or until internal temperature is just over 140°F (60°C).

Remove meat from oven. Transfer from pan to cutting board to rest for 20 minutes.

Deglaze roasting pan with about ¼ cup (60 mL) water, scraping up any browned bits, and drizzle over roast before serving. Slice into rounds about 1½-in (4-cm) thick to serve.

Roasted Baby Potatoes

MAKES 6 SERVINGS

If you are going to the trouble of an elaborate main, I recommend simple and less time-consuming side dishes so that you can focus on what's really important. (For me, that's sneaking more than my fair share of cookies and topping up my wine glass inconspicuously.) I am fond of these potatoes because you can boil them up to three days before—just make sure they are dry and at least room temperature when you roast them. They'll roast alongside your Stuffed Pork Loin (p. 206).

3 lb (1.5 kg) baby or nugget potatoes, scrubbed

2 tbsp kosher salt

¼ cup (125 mL) olive oil

3 tbsp kosher salt, divided

1 lemon, zest and juice

2 tbsp minced fresh mint

1 tbsp minced fresh rosemary

1 tsp crushed red pepper flakes

In a large pot, place potatoes and cover with cold water. Add salt, then bring to a boil on high heat. Boil for 10 minutes, then drain. Spread potatoes out on a baking sheet lined with a clean kitchen towel to cool.

Preheat oven to 325°F (160°C).

Remove kitchen towel, and, spreading potatoes out in a single layer, drizzle with olive oil and sprinkle with salt, shaking around on pan to coat completely.

Roast for 30 minutes, then shake pan to turn potatoes, and roast for another 20–30 minutes.

Sprinkle roasted potatoes with lemon zest, then squeeze juice over top, discarding seeds. Sprinkle mint, rosemary, and red pepper flakes over top. Give pan another quick shake, and spoon potatoes and herbs into a serving dish.

Roast Beef with Wilted Escarole

Roast beef always seems like special-occasion food to me. A simple roast marinated in flavorful soy sauce, mustard, and garlic cooks to medium-rare in under an hour, so that all you really have to worry about is your holiday playlist and making sure your halls are appropriately decked. Ask your butcher to tie the roast so you don't have to. Serve with Luscious Mashed Potatoes (p. 176), grainy Dijon mustard, and store-bought horseradish.

½ cup (125 mL) soy sauce

¼ cup (60 mL) olive oil

2 tsp grainy Dijon mustard

2 tsp ground black pepper, divided

2 garlic cloves, smashed + 2 minced garlic cloves, divided

2.5 lb (1 kg) inside round beef roast

4 tbsp butter, divided

½ cup (125 mL) beer such as pilsner or lager

1 shallot, minced

2 lb (900 g) escarole, rinsed and patted dry

salt, to taste

In a bowl, combine soy sauce, oil, mustard, 1 tsp pepper, and 2 smashed garlic cloves. Place roast in large freezer bag with a zip top; pour soy sauce marinade inside. Seal bag near top of roast to remove air and force marinade around all sides of roast. Marinate at least one hour and up to 24 hours. Bring to room temperature by removing from fridge and letting the meat sit on the counter in the marinade for an hour.

Preheat oven to 325°F (160°C).

In a large frying pan on medium-high heat, melt 2 tbsp butter. Remove roast from marinade, reserving 2 tbsp. Brown roast on all sides, about 2 minutes per side, to develop a crust. Meat should lift easily from pan when it's time to turn—if it sticks, give it a little bit more time.

Add beer and reserved marinade to pan.

Roast for about 45–55 minutes (18–19 minutes per lb [454 g]), turning pan once, midway, for even cooking. Roast will be cooked to medium-rare when internal temperature reaches 125°F (51°C). Medium-cooked beef has an internal temperature of 145°F (60°C). Well-done roast beef is an abomination I cannot condone.

Roast Beef with Wilted Escarole cont'd

When roast is cooked to temperature, remove from oven and set on a plate to rest for 10–15 minutes. Crease a large piece of aluminum foil in the middle to form a tent, and set over beef.

Roughly chop escarole, discarding core.

Return frying pan to stove. On medium-high heat, melt 2 tbsp butter. Add shallots and minced garlic, and sauté for 1 minute, scraping up any browned bits. Add escarole, and cover pan with lid. Steam for 2–3 minutes, until escarole has wilted.

Pour any liquid that has seeped out of beef into pan with escarole. Stir and then taste; adjust seasonings as needed.

Place escarole on a serving platter, and carve roast beef in thin slices. Lay sliced beef over escarole, drizzle with pan juices, and sprinkle 1 tsp pepper over beef.

Red Wine-Braised Cabbage

Cabbage is at its cheapest and most abundant in November and December, which makes it a practical choice for a holiday side dish. It's also very high in fiber, which gives your feasting a bit of balance, and it takes well to festive flavors, like a bit of cinnamon and a bit of wine.

1 red cabbage

4 tbsp butter, divided

2 shallots, halved lengthwise and thinly sliced

2 cups peeled, cored and grated tart green apples, such as Granny Smith

1 cup (250 mL) red wine, such as Merlot

¼ cup (60 mL) brown sugar, packed

½ tsp kosher salt

½ tsp ground black pepper

1 bay leaf

1 cinnamon stick

1 tbsp apple cider vinegar

Remove any damaged outer leaves from cabbage, then halve lengthwise. Cut in half again lengthwise, then cut core from each wedge. Slice each quarter horizontally into thin ribbons. Set aside.

In a large, heavy-bottomed pot on medium-high heat, melt 2 tbsp butter. Add shallots, and cook for 2 minutes. Place grated apples and chopped cabbage into pot and, as best you can, stir to coat. I find that a pair of long tongs works best for this.

Add wine, brown sugar, salt, pepper, bay leaf, and cinnamon stick, and stir to combine. Cover, reduce heat to medium, and cook, removing lid occasionally to stir, for about 20 minutes.

Remove lid, and cook until liquid has mostly dissipated, another 4–6 minutes.

Add 2 tbsp butter and 1 tbsp vinegar, and stir to coat. Cabbage should appear glossy and be soft with a residual bit of crunch. Discard bay leaf and cinnamon stick before serving.

Lettuce Salad with Herbs

The point of this salad is that it is simple—it's meant to cut through rich flavors. Use whichever herbs you have on hand, but I think a bit of dill and tarragon is nice with the mustard dressing; the butter lettuce (sometimes sold as Bibb) is essential.

2 tbsp olive oil

1 tbsp lemon juice

1 tbsp minced shallots (about 1 small shallot)

2 tsp grainy Dijon mustard

1 tsp honey

½ tsp ground black pepper

¼ tsp kosher salt

1 head butter lettuce, cored, leaves roughly torn

¼ cup (60 mL) minced fresh dill

2 tbsp minced fresh tarragon

2 tbsp minced fresh parsley

At the bottom of a large bowl, whisk olive oil, lemon juice, shallots, mustard, honey, pepper, and salt. Pile torn lettuce and minced herbs over top. Refrigerate for up to 30 minutes. Toss just before serving.

Beet & Apple Salad

This slaw is simple, nutritious, and easily made ahead; I cook beets on Sunday night, make this salad, then put it into a bowl to eat later—it's better if it sits overnight. It is especially good as a simple side dish for sausages, or to lend a bit of color to an otherwise brown meal.

4 beets, scrubbed

2 sweet, firm-fleshed apples, such as Ambrosia or Honeycrisp

½ English cucumber

½ cup (250 mL) buttermilk

1 tbsp grainy Dijon mustard

2 tsp honey

1 tsp apple cider vinegar

½ tsp kosher salt

½ tsp ground black pepper

1 tbsp minced fresh tarragon + 1 tbsp whole tarragon leaves

Place whole beets in a pot of cold salted water, and bring to a boil on medium-high heat, simmering for 40–60 minutes, until tender. Fill a bowl with ice water. Drain beets, then plunge into ice water to cool.

When cool enough to handle, slough skins off beets using your fingers and a paring knife, as needed. Dice beets to about ½ in (1 cm).

Core apple, and dice to about ½ in (1 cm).

Dice cucumber to ½ in (1 cm).

In a large bowl, whisk together buttermilk, mustard, honey, vinegar, salt, pepper, and minced tarragon. Add beets, apples, cucumber, and toss to coat. Sprinkle with remaining whole tarragon leaves.

Herring & Potato Salad

This potato salad will be nice to serve at a holiday brunch, perhaps with smoked salmon, soft-boiled eggs, rusks or rye toasts, and a bit of gin and orange juice. It feels restorative, a little briny and salty, but not too virtuous. It's an update on traditional haringsla, which includes many of the ingredients listed below, plus beets and diced apples; if you are nostalgic for that particular combination of flavors, make a bowl of Beet & Apple Salad (p. 214) and serve alongside.

1½ lb (680 g) baby or nugget
  potatoes, halved or quartered
  to bite-sized pieces
4 oz (115 g) marinated or
  pickled herring, diced
½ cup (125 mL) minced dill
  pickles + 2 tbsp pickle brine
4 green onions, chopped
2 celery stalks, finely chopped
2 tbsp chopped fresh dill
2 tbsp olive oil
2 tbsp gin
1 tbsp lemon juice
1 tsp grainy Dijon mustard
½ tsp kosher salt
½ tsp ground black pepper

Place potatoes in a pot of cold salted water and bring to a boil on high heat. Cook for about 15 minutes, until tender, then drain and cool.

Place cooled potatoes in a large bowl, and add diced herring, dill pickles, green onions, celery, and dill.

In a small bowl, combine pickle brine, olive oil, gin, lemon juice, mustard, salt, and pepper. Whisk, then taste and adjust seasonings as needed—remember that pickled herring and dill pickles can be salty.

Pour dressing over salad ingredients and chill for 30 minutes or up to 2 hours. Serve cold.

Rye Poffertjes

Poffertjes are little pancakes, and while you can have them any time of year, they are at their best in December, when the air is a bit cold and a few warm little pancakes at an outdoor Christmas market really hit the spot. Poffertjes are made in a special pan with small round molds so that the pancakes cook into little puffs; if you can't find a poffertje pan, approximate the shape by dropping small rounds of batter into a frying pan instead.

2 cups (500 mL) whole milk

2 tbsp honey

1 tsp dry active yeast

1 cup (250 mL) all-purpose
    flour

1 cup (250 mL) dark rye flour

½ tsp ground cinnamon

½ tsp kosher salt

½ cup (125 mL) melted butter

¼ cup (60 mL) powdered sugar

drizzle of golden syrup

In a saucepan on medium, heat milk to lukewarm, about 100°F (38°C). Whisk in honey, and add yeast. Remove from heat and let rest for 5 minutes, or until yeast froths and appears fluffy.

In a large bowl, combine all-purpose and rye flour, cinnamon, and salt.

Add milk mixture and melted butter, working gently to just combine—do not overwork batter, which will result in tough pancakes.

Cover with plastic wrap and a clean kitchen towel, and let rest in a warm spot for 1 hour.

Set lightly greased poffertje pan on medium heat. Give batter a quick stir to deflate. Working in batches, spoon batter into individual poffertje molds and cook for about 2 minutes per side, until golden. Dust with powdered sugar and drizzle with golden syrup before serving.

Pepper Nuts

Traditionally, Zwarte Piet (see p. 229) arrives with handfuls of pepper nuts—pepernoten—which are tossed to children from the front door of the home. They are a firm, spicy cookie, and when not being thrown at children, they make an excellent accompaniment to a hot cup of coffee. I add a bit of cocoa to mine to complement the traditional spices.

½ cup (125 mL) butter

½ cup (125 mL) brown sugar

1 egg, beaten

1 tbsp Dutch process cocoa

1 tsp anise extract

1 tsp ground ginger

½ tsp ground cinnamon

¼ tsp ground cloves

¼ tsp ground nutmeg

2 cups (500 mL) all-purpose flour

1 tsp baking powder

½ tsp kosher salt

Preheat oven to 350°F (175°C). Line a baking sheet with parchment. Set aside.

In a large bowl, cream together butter and sugar. Add egg and beat until fluffy. Scrape down sides of bowl, add cocoa, anise extract, ginger, cinnamon, cloves, and nutmeg, and beat until well-combined. Scrape down sides of bowl again.

In a separate bowl, whisk together flour, baking powder, and salt. Gradually add dry ingredients to butter mixture until mixture appears crumbly. Add cold water, 1 tbsp at a time (up to 3 tbsp) until mixture forms a dough.

Use your hands to roll into ¾-in (2-cm) balls—a little bigger than a marble. Set on prepared baking sheet about 1 in (2.5 cm) apart.

Bake for 15 minutes, then remove to a wire rack to cool. Store in sealed container for up to a week.

Sugar

"In all manner of confectionery and pastry these people excelled; and having fruit in great abundance, which costs them nothing, and getting sugar home at an easy rate from the West Indies, the quantity of these articles used in families, otherwise plain and frugal, was astonishing." —Anne MacVicar Grant, *Memoirs of an American Lady* (1808)

"But the great enemy, a tireless worker for Satan, was sugar." —Simon Schama, The Embarrassment of Riches: *An Interpretation of Dutch Culture in the Golden Age* (1997)

Dutch people love sugar. They love it so much! When I began to research the cuisine of the Netherlands, I always thought it was funny how many recipes these old books had for pastries, pancakes, and sweets. The ratio in some cases was 2:1; one 1972 cookbook contains just one recipe for chicken, but six for pudding. And not "pudding" in the generic, all-dessert-encompassing British sense—I mean actual pudding.

My favorite part of Dutch supermarkets is the aisle for sandwich spreads. They have peanut butter and jam, but they also have Nutella and an infinite variety of chocolate spreads—white, milk, and dark—and speculaas spreads and coconut spreads, and it goes on and on and on. There are also innumerable varieties of hagelslaag (sprinkles) and vlokken (chocolate shavings served to children on buttered bread at breakfast). I am pretty sure that there were more sweet things that you could put on bread than there were kinds of packaged soup. I felt very at home in the Netherlands. The World Health Organization recommends that daily sugar consumption should not exceed five percent of calories per day—that's about twenty-five grams or six teaspoons of sugar—for an adult of average size. In the Netherlands, the average adult eats about 102.5 grams of sugar per day.

The Dutch taste for sugar has always been noteworthy—it was something that the Calvinist church viewed as dangerous as far back as the Golden Age, even as it acknowledged that sugar was a difficult vice to reign in, as it was abundant, cheap, and even commoners had access to it. It was the Dutch who drove Caribbean sugar production and trade, essentially monopolizing the sugar trade in the seventeenth century. Dutch merchants were uniquely able to support producers through credit, offering an upfront investment in capital, labor, and machinery to sugar producers in exchange for the rights to export and sell harvests. At one point, the Dutch were bringing as many as 3,000 African and Asian slaves a year to the Caribbean, Suriname, and Brazil exclusively for sugar harvesting and production. By the mid-1600s, there were more than fifty sugar refineries operating in Amsterdam alone. Today, Dutch sugar primarily comes from sugar beets, which accounts for roughly twelve percent of Dutch agricultural land use.

In 1990, a study from researchers at the Katholieke Universiteit te Nijmegen found that "despite the existence of a fair amount of knowledge about the relation of sugar consumption and dental health, the main part of the ... population does not belief in the effectiveness of sugar avoidance in the preservation of the teeth. As an average, the ... Dutch take, apart from the meals, nearly eight sugar-containing products a day" (online at https://www.ncbi.nlm.nih.gov/pubmed/2130278). Anecdotally, this holds true for Nick's family; Nick's great-aunt once said that if her teeth rotted from eating too much sugar, she would simply get dentures.

sugar ....

One of my fondest moments in Haarlem was stumbling upon a "gebak" stand where piles of fresh-made doughnuts were illuminated and bathed in golden light; they glowed against the grey backdrop of a winter day. You could have olliebollen, plain or with raisins, or apple bollen, fresh doughnuts filled with spiced, sweet apple compote, or a variation with oozy chocolate filling. Many of the doughnuts had already been rolled in sugar, but if you wanted, you could have your doughnut plopped into a heap of confectioner's sugar; of course, we wanted. As Hunter bit into his doughnut, a cloud of icing sugar blew up around him, covering his toque and coat and scarf and the bottoms of his pants and the tops of his shoes. He is not a kid who likes to be dirty, but in a brief moment I watched as he appeared to consider the mess and then proceed in spite of it, savoring that doughnut for a long, long time and being quiet the whole while. "Is this Dutch snow?" he asked, once he had finished his doughnut and finally noticed that he had become sugar-coated. "I think it is," I said, and I stand by it.

Jan Hagel Cookies

MAKES 30 COOKIES

These are a bit like Dutch shortbread, and are served around the holidays. The recipe—and whether these are cut after baking (like shortbread) or baked into individual cookies—differs from family to family. I like them as individual cookies. "Hagel" means hail, and these are meant to have a hail-like smattering of chopped nuts on each cookie; traditionally, this would mean almonds, but combining almonds and pistachios lends a more festive feel.

½ lb (250 g) room-temperature butter

½ cup (125 mL) + 2 tbsp granulated sugar, divided

1 egg, separated

½ tsp almond extract

2 cups (500 mL) all-purpose flour

½ tsp ground cinnamon

¼ tsp kosher salt

¼ cup (60 mL) finely chopped slivered almonds

¼ cup (60 mL) finely chopped shelled pistachios

Preheat oven to 375°F (190°C).

In a stand mixer or in a large bowl using a handheld mixer, cream butter and ½ cup sugar together. Scrape sides of bowl down, then add egg yolk and almond extract. Beat for about 10 minutes, until fluffy, and sugar has mostly dissolved.

In a bowl, combine flour, cinnamon, and salt, then add to wet ingredients and mix until just combined.

In a small bowl, combine almonds and pistachios. Set aside.

Beat egg white with 1 tbsp water until foamy. Set aside.

Roll dough into 1-in (2.5-cm) balls, and place roughly 1.5-in (4-cm) apart on parchment paper-lined baking sheet. Flatten each ball with the tines of a fork.

Brush each cookie with egg white mixture.

Sprinkle 1 tbsp sugar over cookies, then carefully spoon about 1 tsp nuts into fork indentations. Gently press down on nuts to push into each cookie. Repeat with second batch of sugar and nuts.

Bake for 15–20 minutes, until golden. Cool on a wire rack. Store in a sealed container for up to 5 days, or make ahead and freeze for up to 1 month.

Caribbean Macaroons

Flaky coconut dressed in what is essentially a puddle of coconut fudge is a great way to satisfy your holiday craving for pure, unadulterated sugar.

7 oz (200 g) large flake (unsweetened) coconut
2 cups (500 mL) brown sugar
14 oz (398 mL) can coconut cream
1 tbsp dark rum
½ tsp ground cinnamon
½ tsp kosher salt

Line a large baking sheet with parchment paper.

Toast coconut until golden and fragrant. If using a microwave, place coconut in a microwave-safe pie plate. Cook on high for 1 minute, stir, and continue to cook and stir for 3–4 minutes, until golden.

Or, preheat oven to 350°F (175°C). Spread coconut in a single layer on a baking sheet and toast in oven for 10 minutes, stirring occasionally, until golden. Remove toasted coconut to a large mixing bowl, and set aside.

In a saucepan on medium heat, combine brown sugar and coconut cream, and heat to 240°F (115°C), whisking occasionally, for about 40 minutes. Note: these will set differently in high humidity; if it is a humid or rainy day, cook sugar and coconut cream mixture to 245°F (118°C) to compensate for moisture in the air.

Whisk in rum, cinnamon, and salt, and pour over coconut, stirring to coat. Working quickly, spoon 24 equal mounds of coconut onto prepared baking sheet. Cool completely, then store in a jar with a tight-fitting lid. These will keep for up to 1 week.

Honey Rice Pudding

MAKES 6 SERVINGS

This rijstebrij (rice pudding) is a nice way to end a rich meal or, if you're on winter break, a sweet way to start the day. Rice pudding is a traditional treat that's often served on Christmas Eve, but this is nice any time you've got company. If you're feeling festive, serve it with Brandied Raisins (opposite).

½ cup (125 mL) long-grain
    white rice
¼ tsp kosher salt
1 tbsp butter
½ cup (125 mL) honey
2 cups (500 mL) cold whole
    milk
1 tsp vanilla extract
1 cup (250 mL) whipping cream
¼ cup (60 mL) toasted and
    finely chopped unshelled
    pistachios

In a saucepan on medium-high heat, bring rice, salt, and 1 cup (250 mL) water to a boil. Cover, then reduce heat to low and cook for 15 minutes. Remove saucepan from heat, and place rice in a bowl. (You can do this step up to 2 days in advance—store covered in refrigerator until ready to use.)

Return pan to stove and bring heat up to medium-high. Melt butter. Add honey and cook for about 1 minute, until it melts and is bubbly.

Add milk, vanilla, and rice. Bring mixture to a boil, then reduce heat to medium and, stirring occasionally, simmer for 30–40 minutes, until liquid has reduced and thickened and mixture has a loose, porridge-like texture.

Pour rice mixture into bowl, cover, and refrigerate for about 2 hours, until cool.

In a separate bowl, beat whipping cream for about 7 minutes, until it forms soft peaks.

Stir about a third of whipped cream into rice mixture. With a spatula, gently fold remainder of whipped cream into rice mixture until incorporated.

Divide between 6 bowls, top with chopped toasted pistachios, and serve immediately.

Brandied Raisins

Known as boerenjongens, which translates to "farm boys," this is a bit like a dried fruit rumtopf (a German dessert served at Christmas). I don't love raisins, so I've made this with dried cranberries and it's very good; with dried apricots and a bit of lemon peel, it's known as boerenmeisjes, or "farm girls." Make this at least three months ahead and store in the refrigerator until the holidays. We use the dried fruit as a dessert topping and the fruit-infused brandy as an aperitif.

1 cinnamon stick

8 whole cloves

½ cup (125 mL) brown sugar

3 cups (750 mL) sultana raisins

2 ½ cups (625 mL) brandy

Place cinnamon stick and cloves in a 1-qt (1-L) jar with a tight-fitting lid.

In a saucepan on medium heat, combine sugar with 1 cup (250 mL) water and bring to a gentle boil to dissolve sugar. Add raisins and cover. Turn off heat and let pot sit, covered, for 10 minutes.

Stir in brandy. Pour raisin-brandy mixture over cinnamon stick and cloves in jar. Seal jar with lid. Store in a cool, dry place or refrigerate for at least 3 and up to 6 months.

Buttermilk Olliebollen

The best thing about these is that they are not beholden to a specific form—they are literally pinched-off hunks of dough; no shaping or finessing needed. Olliebollen are a very forgiving introduction to the world of at-home doughnut cookery. Make these traditional New Year's Eve treats for your next party, and everyone will think you're some kind of miraculous kitchen wizard. I believe in you. You are. Now go forth and fry.

1 tbsp honey

1 tsp dry active yeast

2 cups (500 mL) buttermilk

1 large navel orange, zest and
   juice

½ tsp ground nutmeg

1 cup (250 mL) dried
   unsweetened cranberries

½ cup (125 mL) minced
   candied ginger

2 cups (500 mL) all-purpose
   flour

½ tsp kosher salt

4–6 cups (1–1.5 L) canola or
   other neutral oil, for frying

¼ cup (60 mL) confectioner's
   sugar

In a large mixing bowl, combine 2 tbsp lukewarm water, honey, and yeast. Let stand for 5 minutes, until yeast begins to foam and look fluffy.

Whisk in buttermilk, orange zest and juice, nutmeg, cranberries, and ginger. Add flour and salt, and mix to form a shaggy dough—somewhere between a batter and a dough. Knead as best you can, or mix in a stand mixer fitted with a dough hook for about 6 minutes, or until dough feels stretchy.

Cover bowl with plastic wrap and a clean kitchen towel. Let stand in a warm place until doubled in size, about 1 hour.

Fill a large, heavy-bottomed pot with oil. On high, heat oil to 375°F (190° C). Pinch balls of dough directly from mixing bowl and drop into hot oil, a few at a time. Use caution when working around hot oil! Move balls and flip with a slotted metal spoon for even cooking. Cook for 4–6 minutes, until golden, then remove to a plate lined with paper towels.

When all olliebollen are fried, transfer to a serving dish and sprinkle with confectioner's sugar shaken from above through a fine-mesh sieve.

Sinterklaas and Zwarte Piet

Please don't get me wrong: I am all for scaring children, especially at Christmas. And while we are not an "Elf on the Shelf," "this-apartment-is-a-surveillance-state-and-you-must-comply-or-else" family, I have been known to threaten the dark, unspoken implications of finding one-self on Santa's naughty list. For kids with dot-ing grandmothers and generous aunties, "no presents from Santa" is not a valid threat—they know there's a payoff waiting for them regard-less of how well they held their act together in front of their parents all December long. For those kids, for my son, a hint of holiday horror is a much more effective way to guarantee good behavior during those cold weeks of December when everyone's eaten too much sugar and spent too much time together indoors.

In the alpine countries of Europe, Krampus (what I like to call Christmas Satan) punishes and kidnaps badly behaved children. Krampus is one of those Germanic, pagan traditions that was absorbed by Christianity as it spread through Europe. But when he fell out of favor with those who felt his likeness to the actual devil was may-be a bit much, exhausted parents everywhere realized they would need something to keep the threat of punishment alive for their chil-dren. This is how we ended up with Santa Claus, though in his early incarnation he was someone who would reward good children and interrogate and beat bad children—which, if you think about it, is even more frightening because the outcome is unpredictable if you are not certain whether you were good or bad.

In the low countries (Belgium and the Neth-erlands), a different sort of threat existed in the form of Black Pete.

The Christmas season begins in the Nether-lands with the celebration of Sinterklaas, a San-ta Claus-like figure who arrives bearing gifts, delivering these throughout the country over the month of December. Christmas proper is not a gift-giving occasion for many families, and so for children, Sinterklaas is the main event. On December 5, Sinterklaas arrives in Amsterdam by boat from Spain with his, um, helper: Zwarte Piet, or Black Pete.

Black Pete is a little like one of Santa's elves, except that he is also a blackface caricature. Black Pete's origin story has become muddled. In the original story, he's a Moor from Spain. The Moors were Muslims from North Africa who conquered the Iberian Peninsula in Spain and Portugal in the sixth century and ruled there for 800 years. It was the Moors who introduced Arabic numbers to Europe and brought many of the spices, dried fruits, and other products—in-cluding rice and fabrics—that would later ex-cite most of the continent. Muslim Moors were expelled from Spain by the Catholic monarchy during the Spanish Inquisition, which began in 1478; only those who would convert to Christian-ity could stay. About 3,000 people were execut-ed during the Inquisition, and the tribunal under which the Inquisition maintained its power was not disbanded until 1834.

That Black Pete began as a black Moor from Spain is significant—the Moors remained a specter in the European imagination long after the Inquisition. Black Pete, in the beginning, was meant to be a fearsome character, carrying a switch and the looming threat of stuffing bad children in a sack and kidnapping them back to Spain. In 1850, while slavery was still going on in the Dutch holding of Suriname, a Dutch schoolteacher published *Sint-Nikolaas en zijn knecht*, a children's story about Sinterklaas and his servant Zwarte Piet. Over time, more Black Petes were added; Sinterklaas now travels with an entourage. Tellingly, Zwarte Piet was not thought to have been adopted in the North American Dutch colonies. In New Amsterdam, the descendants of Dutch settlers had Grumpus, thought to be related to Krampus, whose traditions do not seem to include blackface—Grumpus (or Black Peter) wears a black eye mask instead.

By 1950, Black Pete's origins were largely rewritten, and he was thought to be a chimneysweep—his blackness was explained as soot (though there is little explanation for his Afro or exaggerated red lips). Generations of children have heard this version of the story, and in modern times Black Pete is no longer a terrifying figure but a benevolent assistant to Sinterklaas.

Please don't get me wrong: I am all for scaring children

He tosses handfuls of pepernoten—Pepper Nuts (p. 219)—to children and is generally a jovial, playful figure. In a 2013 story in the New Yorker, professor Peter Jan Margry of the University of Amsterdam explained that "Dutch defenders of the tradition have trouble seeing Black Pete as a racist figure because they like him so much, and have for so many generations." Because generations of children have experienced Black Pete as a fun, lovable character, they have not been cognizant of his history and have accepted the chimneysweep narrative.

It's not hard to understand, given how Black Pete looks in many celebrations across the Netherlands, that some black Dutch people would find the caricature unsettling. When you understand the history of the character, it's also not hard to agree that there is an undercurrent of racial bias, to say the least. And it's important to really hear black voices when they are saying that Black Pete is not okay.

In a 2016 video on the website Vox.com, Mieke Bal, professor at the University of Amsterdam (who received a royal commendation and was appointed Knight of the Order of the Netherlands Lion in 2017 for her contribution to Dutch cultural understanding) explains what Black Pete meant to her: "I remember vividly the sentiment of being scared," Bal says, "the terror of young children, who don't feel safe. It's an emotion that stays with you … If you habituate children to this response to these strange characters with black faces, that's their model of black people."

The Dutch population is eighty percent white.

If you are going to terrify or otherwise mislead children, in my experience it's best to do it with a figure who is not real so that you can take it back later if you have to (like when they get night terrors, oops). Black Pete, to children, is very real—he looks like a parody of a black man. Again, in my experience, young children are not great with nuance—they accept what they are told, even in jest, and they trust that you're telling them real, true things, which is why you have to be so careful. Over the past few years, protests have taken place during the arrival of Sinterklaas and Black Pete, with arrests and violence marring an otherwise festive occasion. People are upset about Black Pete, and that's absolutely fair; people are also upset that people are upset about Black Pete, which is to be expected. Though I am sure people mean well, it's sometimes hard to think critically about our dearly held traditions. And so, even as we must move forward, there will always be people looking back.

But things are changing because Sinterklaas is supposed to be a celebration, and it is meant for everyone. For the past few years, people have increasingly preferred to adopt the chimneysweep narrative. Parade organizers and television show producers have moved away from blackface and have renamed Black Pete "Chimney Pete." If he really is a chimneysweep, then there is no need for racial stereotypes (or facepaint); he just has a bit of soot on his face and that's it. Then anyone can be Chimney Pete, and everyone can enjoy him. And if we are going to tell the children that he is a kind, if dirty, man who just slid out of a chimney to throw cookies on their floors, then we can certainly dress him properly to play the part. It's the holidays, and aren't the holidays a lot more memorable when everyone's included and no one is left out in the cold?

Bishop's Wine

Every year, my mom and I go to the Vancouver Christmas Market, in theory to see holiday stuff, but in reality, to drink mulled wine and spend a lot of money on artisanal soap. The Dutch version of mulled wine is similar to what we get at the Christmas market—a little wine, a little citrus, some spice, and just enough kick to get you into the holiday spirit.

Tip: Chilean red wines are often inexpensive but good quality.

2 24-oz (750-mL) bottles of
    Cabernet Sauvignon
½ cup (125 mL) brandy
½ cup (125 mL) orange juice
½ cup (125 mL) brown sugar,
    packed
1 navel orange, sliced into
    rounds
1 lemon, sliced into rounds
10 whole cloves
4 whole star anise
2 cinnamon sticks

Place all ingredients in a large pot on medium-low heat and simmer—but do not boil—for 2 hours. If it starts to boil, remove from heat for a few minutes, reduce heat, and return pot to burner to continue simmering.

Alternatively, place all ingredients in a slow cooker on low, and simmer for up to 6 hours.

Before serving, remove orange and lemon slices and spices. To serve, ladle into mugs.

CONDIMENTS
& PRESERVES

CONDIMENTS & PRESERVES

One of the pleasures of simple, minimally processed food is the condiments. Maybe a plate of mashed potatoes and kale doesn't sound like much, but when it's potatoes and kale and applesauce and hot sauce and mustard, things get a bit more interesting. The Dutch dinner plate is a canvas, and the condiments are what bring it to life.

One of Nick's most endearing qualities is his predilection toward what he calls a "sauce line-up." If there are dips to be had, Nick will have all the dips, which at first I didn't totally appreciate. I understand much better now that I've been preparing our dinners for the past ten years. Nick doesn't like a lot of repetition, but also I am very busy and very tired and somehow end up doing most of the cooking. You know what changes a meal from something you had last week to something totally different today? Condiments.

We maintain a stash of condiments that, at its most basic, includes: between twelve and eighteen different kinds of mustards; an assortment of hot sauces; and a variety of

pickles, including dill pickles, pickled onions, capers, and pickled hot peppers. We have a ridiculous amount of food-adjacent toppings and sauces, even when we have no actual food. This is mostly fine because, in a pinch, a protein plus a vinaigrette and a steamed vegetable is a delicious dinner.

This section contains mainly things you'd pair with other recipes in the book; here, there's a recipe for an applesauce you can serve with anything, a quick ketjap manis that will work if you can't find it in stores or if you need to make it gluten-free; and a couple of sambals you can whip up to impress dinner guests at your next rijsttafel feast.

Canning Sauces, Jams & Jellies

Several of the recipes that follow will suit water-bath canning, a simple, straightforward approach that will not require pressure cooking.

Canning is easy to do and fairly intuitive when you get used to doing it, but you have to understand the basics. The most important thing about water-bath canning is cleanliness—you must make sure your jars, lids, and rings are sterile before you begin.

Fill a canning pot or large stock pot with cold water and set on a large burner on high heat. Put jars in pot and bring to a boil. Let boil for 10 minutes. Put rings in a small saucepan and boil for 10 minutes as well. Do not boil snap lids with rubber rings—these need only to be gently heated. Heating for too long or at too high a temperature can reduce the quality of the seal; a bad seal means a lot of wasted time when your food spoils. Don't waste food.

Be sure to follow recipes precisely to ensure an adequate balance of acidity and sugar; sugar and acids function as preservatives, working in combination with the high heat of water bath canning to neutralize and destroy harmful bacteria and yeasts.

Applesauce

Applesauce—appelmoes—has been part of Dutch cuisine since medieval times. Early recipes used almonds, spices, and fish liver for a paste I can't really imagine; we didn't test such a recipe in preparing this book, but if you're keen, you can track down the recipe in *Wel ende edelike spijse—Good and Noble Food*, a cookery book from the fifteenth century.

Modern recipes for Dutch applesauce often call for Goudreinet apples, a variety that's not widely available in North America outside of a select few regions; it's a sweet, dry apple that's commonly used in sauces, jellies, and baking. I have tried a number of apples for sauce and have settled on Ambrosia, a crisp, sweet variety that keeps its shape in baking and leaves applesauce tasting fresh and bright. Similar apples, such as Honeycrisp, Pink Lady, Gala, or Braeburn, have also worked well for us in the past; any of these will make a sauce that doesn't need a lot of added sugar. You can use sour apples if you prefer, but I find that Granny Smith and other green apples lend an odd tinge to the final product if you cook them with their skins on, and I am too lazy to not do that.

The recipe that follows requires 10 lb (4.5 kg) of apples to produce around 18 cups (4.25 L) of sauce. You can easily halve this recipe, but I find that 10 lb is the minimum I'm willing to put in the effort for—I buy apples in 10-lb (4.5 kg) bags or 25-lb (11.5 kg) boxes from a local farm at clear-out prices before end of season, and the sauce that results keeps us well-stocked throughout the winter. You can make less—10 pounds of apples is a little more than will fit in my biggest pot, and that may be the case for you as well; if you're committed to making the full recipe, you may need to use two pots. Remember to add about a cup (250 mL) of water to each pot, and ensure each has a tight-fitting lid. I prefer canning my applesauce, but it also freezes well.

I also recommend a food mill, especially if you're making a large quantity of sauce. A food mill makes quick work of puréeing the apples, and you don't have to peel or core them to pass them through the mill; it leaves the seeds, inedible bits, and peels behind. It also creates a nice smooth texture, which is especially important if you are feeding the sauce to babies or using it in baking. A simple food mill will cost between $25 and $50 USD, but will save a lot of time; I process ten pounds of apples through my food mill in ten minutes. It is also useful for canning tomatoes, creating silky vegetable soups, and making the best mashed potatoes you've ever had (p. 176).

If you don't have a food mill, you can still make a smooth sauce, but you'll need to peel and core the apples before steaming, and purée with an immersion blender once the apples are tender. If you like a chunky sauce, you can mash the steamed apples with a potato masher.

Simple Canned Applesauce

·············· MAKES 9 PINT (500-ML) JARS ··············

It doesn't matter if my mother-in-law is serving curried chicken or Christmas ham, there's always applesauce on the table. I thought it was just because Nick's dad likes it. But applesauce is to the Dutch dinner plate as ketchup is to Hunter's—essential, unquestionable, and ubiquitous; it's both a condiment and the glue that holds a meal together.

10 lb (4.5 kg) firm-fleshed sweet apples, such as Ambrosia

1 cup (250 mL) granulated sugar

¼ cup (60 mL) lemon juice

Fill a large canning pot with water. Fill pot with clean canning jars, cover, and set to high heat on a back burner. This pot will both sterilize empty jars and process filled ones for canning. Sterilize spoons, jar rings, and other canning equipment in a separate pot of boiling water.

Meanwhile, scrub apples. Discard any with nicks or soft spots. If using a food mill, chop each apple into 1-in (2.5-cm) chunks, and put into a large pot.

If not using a food mill, peel and core apples before chopping them and placing them in pot.

Add 1 cup (250 mL) cold water to pot, cover, and on medium-high heat, cook for 20 minutes or until apples are tender.

Suspend food mill over a large bowl and process apples in batches, discarding peels and core bits that build up. If not using food mill, purée or mash apples in the pot. After either approach, add sugar and lemon juice. Taste, adjusting flavors as needed.

Remove jars from canning pot. Use caution—they will be hot. Carefully spoon sauce into each one, stirring to ensure no air pockets form. Run a clean butter knife around inside of jar to release trapped air. Gently (and using oven mitts), lift each jar slightly before firmly setting it back down. Wipe off any applesauce that may have run down jar. Add lids and secure with rings tightened just until resistance is met. Return jars to canning pot and cover. Boil for 20 minutes.

Simple Canned Applesauce cont'd

Meanwhile, lay a clean kitchen towel on counter or table. Remove jars (again, using caution!) from pot, and gently place on towel. Let stand, untouched, for 24 hours. Once cool, mark the date and store them in a cool dry place for up to 1 year.

Fancy applesauce (variation)
Complete recipe as follows, but add 1 tsp vanilla extract or scraped contents of 1 vanilla bean pod when adding sugar and lemon juice.

Cinnamon applesauce (variation)
Complete recipe as follows, but replace half the granulated sugar with brown sugar, and add 1 tsp ground cinnamon when adding sugar and lemon juice.

Appelstroop

Appelstroop—more of a jelly than a jam—has dark, smoky flavors from the molasses and tastes almost savory. It's delicious with a bit of ham and cheese on bread for breakfast; it's also nice as part of a charcuterie plate. To can appelstroop for longer storage (or for gifts), process as per canning instructions on p. 234.

7 cups (1.7 L) apple cider or
unsweetened apple juice
1 cup (250 mL) molasses
2 tbsp lemon juice

In a large saucepan on medium heat, combine apple cider, molasses, and lemon juice. Simmer slowly, skimming off foam that forms on surface and whisking occasionally, for 40–60 minutes. Bring to between 220°F (104°C)–230°F (110°C).

Don't rush it—if it gets too hot, it will turn into taffy, not be spreadable, and you may not be able to get it out of the jars. You will know when it's getting close—the mixture will boil up into big, frothy bubbles. Do not let it boil over.

Pour into a quart (1-L) canning jar and let cool to room temperature. Cover with a tight-fitting lid, and store in refrigerator for up to 1 month.

Rosy Rhubarb Preserve

Rhubarb was not particularly popular in the Netherlands until the late twentieth century, but it was adopted by Dutch immigrants to Canada and the US. Now, many Dutch-Canadian family gardens include a hardy, perennial rhubarb plant (most likely bought from a Dutch nursery, which, where I live at least, is most of them). This is a thrifty way to stretch your backyard rhubarb harvest. It's particularly tasty served with Currant Bread (p. 35).

Tip: If you intend to can rhubarb preserves for long-term storage, follow sterilization procedure detailed in recipe for applesauce (p. 240).

5 lb (2.25 kg) rhubarb
4 cups (1 L) sugar
¼ cup (60 mL) lemon juice
1 tbsp rose water

Fill a large pot with rhubarb and sugar, tossing to coat. Let stand for 30 minutes to draw some of the liquid out of rhubarb before cooking.

Set pot on medium heat and add lemon juice. Stirring occasionally, bring rhubarb up to about 220°F (105°C) for 40–50 minutes.

Stir in rose water, and adjust seasonings to taste.

Ladle into jars. If canning, wipe rims and run a knife around the inside of the jar to remove trapped pockets of air. Tighten rings around the lids just until resistance is met.

Process in a hot-water bath for 20 minutes. Remove jars from pot and let stand at room temperature for 24 hours.

Dried Apricot Jam

My son Hunter is fond of this jam as a topping for waffles; I like it on toasted Sugar Bread (p. 39) for breakfast. When you see dried apricots on sale, it's time to make this.

Tip: If you intend to can for long-term storage, follow sterilization procedure detailed in recipe for applesauce (p. 240).

1 lb (454 g) dried apricots
2 cinnamon sticks
10 whole cloves
4 cups (1 L) granulated sugar
1 cup (250 mL) orange juice
½ cup (125 mL) brandy
¼ cup (60 mL) lemon juice

Roughly chop apricots. In a large bowl, combine with cinnamon sticks and whole cloves. Cover with 4 cups (1 L) boiling water. Let sit overnight, or for up to 12 hours.

Discard cloves and cinnamon sticks, then pour apricots and water into a saucepan with sugar, orange juice, brandy, and lemon juice. Cook, uncovered, on medium heat for 40–50 minutes, until mixture reaches 220°F (105°C) and apricots begin to dissolve.

Ladle into sterilized canning jars. If canning, wipe glasses and run a knife around inside of jar to remove any trapped air pockets. Tighten rings around lids just until resistance is met.

Process in a hot-water bath for 20 minutes. Remove jars from pot and let stand at room temperature for 24 hours.

Ketjap Manis

Ketjap manis (also spelled kecap manis) is a hugely important ingredient in Indonesian and Indo-Dutch cuisine. It's a thick, sweet soy sauce that's fundamental to a great many dishes, including those in this book. I generally buy ABC Brand ketjap manis from a local bodega, but it's hard to come by in some locations. This recipe can be made gluten-free; look for gluten-free soy sauce in gourmet stores or Asian supermarkets (or even, sometimes, Walmart). If you have ever made a reduction of balsamic vinegar, this process will be familiar.

3 cups (750 mL) soy sauce

3 cups (750 mL) brown sugar, packed

2 tbsp molasses

4 whole star anise

In a saucepan on medium-high heat, whisk together soy sauce, brown sugar, and molasses. Add star anise, and bring to a boil before reducing heat to medium; simmer for about 20 minutes, until sugar has dissolved and sauce has reduced by half and thickened to a syrup.

Remove star anise and discard. Pour sauce into a jar with a tight-fitting lid, and store at room temperature for up to 1 month.

Garlic Mayonnaise

Dutch frietsaus—fry sauce—is basically mayonnaise, just a bit lower in fat. Serve this as a dip for Dutch Fries (p. 98), for Paprika Bitterballs (p. 80), and as the base for a tartar sauce for Kibbeling (p. 96). It is also great on sandwiches with leftover roast beef (p. 210). Please note that this recipe uses raw egg. Raw eggs can occasionally be contaminated with salmonella, and consuming raw eggs can be risky for young children, pregnant women, and people with compromised immune systems. Just be careful, okay?

1½ cups (625 mL) canola or other neutral oil

4 garlic cloves, divided

1 egg

2 tbsp white wine vinegar

1 tbsp grainy Dijon mustard

½ tsp salt

Preheat oven to 400°F (200°C).

Fill a baking dish with oil, then smash 2 garlic cloves and place in oil. Bake for about 25 minutes, until garlic is deeply golden and has infused oil. Discard garlic cloves, and let oil stand until cool.

In a stand blender, add egg, vinegar, mustard, and salt with 2 garlic cloves. If blender lid has a cap in the middle, remove cap; if there's a vent, open vent. Begin to blend, and gently pour oil into blender in a thin stream. Continue blending to emulsify. Taste and adjust seasonings as needed. Serve immediately, or store in refrigerator for up to 3 days.

Hangop

Hangop gets its name from the fact that, at one point, buttermilk or yogurt were hung up in a clean towel or pillowcase to strain off the whey, leaving the milk solids behind. This mixture is thick and is either sweetened or eaten plain; there seem to be as many ways to make it as there are households that enjoy it. I make mine with a mix of yogurt and buttermilk, and leave it on the counter overnight to thicken a bit. Choose a yogurt with 3–6 percent fat that contains only milk ingredients and bacterial cultures; no gelatins, no starches.

3 cups (750 mL) unflavored natural yogurt
2 tbsp full-fat buttermilk

Line a fine-mesh sieve with cheesecloth, a clean dish towel, or paper towel, and position over a medium-sized bowl. Place yogurt in sieve and let drain for 30–60 minutes. Remove to a bowl, and stir in buttermilk. Let stand, partially covered, at room temperature, for 24 hours.

Stores for up to 2 weeks in refrigerator.

Blender Peanut Sauce

This peanut sauce will work as a dressing for Gado Gado (p. 153), or as a dipping sauce for Chicken Sate (p. 154). If you stir equal amounts Garlic Mayonnaise (p. 247) and this peanut sauce together, you will have an excellent sauce for Dutch Fries (p. 98).

1 shallot, minced

2 tbsp fresh ginger, minced

2 garlic cloves, smashed

1 cup (250 mL) creamy peanut
butter

¾ cup (175 mL) coconut milk

2 tbsp fish sauce

2 tbsp ketjap manis

1 tbsp lemon juice

1 tbsp sambal oelek

½ tsp ground black pepper

In a stand blender, combine shallots, ginger, and garlic with ½ cup (125 mL) boiling water. Let stand for 5 minutes.

Add peanut butter, coconut milk, fish sauce, ketjap manis, lemon juice, sambal oelek, and pepper, and blend until smooth. Adjust seasonings to taste.

Store in a sealed jar in refrigerator for up to 1 week.

Curry Ketchup

Curry ketchup is a little sweeter than regular ketchup, and it's brown. It reminds me a bit of HP Sauce, and it goes well with sausages, fries, and on sandwiches with leftover Braised Meatballs (p. 122).

1 cup (250 mL) ketchup

2 tbsp ketjap manis

1 tsp yellow curry powder

In a bowl, whisk together ketchup, ketjap manis, and curry powder. Store in a sealed jar in refrigerator for up to 1 month.

Sambals

If you are buying sambal oelek, Huy Fong makes a good one; they're based in Los Angeles and use red jalapeño peppers. Do not feel like you have to use one kind of pepper to make your sambals, as if there is but one way to do these kinds of things. I generally make my sambal oelek out of red habañero peppers—known in Indonesia as adjuma—that I buy from a local farm where they are cheap in mid-autumn.

You can make sambals raw or cooked; I make my sambal oelek out of lacto-fermented peppers because—as my friend Katherine says—I'm a weird hippie. Make sambals in small amounts to serve fresh, and buy commercial varieties to use in cooking. If you are sensitive to heat, halve peppers lengthwise and scrape out the seeds and the inner membrane (the spongy innards the seeds are stuck to), which is where most of the spicy taste is.

Sambal Oelek

A sambal is an Indonesian chili sauce used in cooking and as a condiment. Sambal oelek is more Dutch than Indonesian, made from raw chilies and salt, and that's about it. I usually make a batch of sambal oelek in fall when chilies are at their peak, but I never manage to make as much as we use.

1 lb (454 g) red habanero
    peppers
1 tsp kosher salt

Remove stems from chilies. In a food processor, grind peppers and salt until a paste forms. Or, chop chilies finely with a large knife, add to bowl, and mix in salt.

Serve fresh or store in refrigerator for up to 1 month.

Green Sambal

Green sambal is made with green chili peppers—serranos or jalapeños work well here. Serve green sambal with rijsttafel, but if you have extra, throw it in a pan with 2 tbsp canola oil and either six hardboiled eggs or 1 lb (454 g) of white fish, such as sole. Serve over rice.

1 lb (454 g) jalapeño peppers
2 shallots
6 garlic cloves
½ packed cup (125 mL) fresh
    cilantro, stems included
2 limes, zest and juice
2 tsp kosher salt

Pre-heat broiler to high.

Place peppers, shallots, and garlic on a baking sheet or pie plate, and broil for about 6 minutes, until just charred. Turn and broil for an additional 4–6 minutes, until just charred on both sides.

Remove stems from chilies and discard. In a food processor or blender, combine mixture with cilantro and grind, or chop finely with a large knife. Mix in lime zest and juice and salt.

RESOURCES

If you'd like to learn more about what makes the Dutch so ... well, Dutch, I've compiled a selected list of further reading. A couple of the books are out of print, but request them from your local library! They're out there, and they're worth checking out.

WEBSITES

www.coquinaria.nl

Coquinaria is a labor of love from Dutch writer and food historian Christianne Muusers. Of her site, Christianne says: "Coquinaria is not slick, commercial, or trendy. I'll leave it at that," but it's home to a wealth of information about the origins of ingredients and recipes in the Dutch canon. The site is invaluable if you hope to understand medieval Dutch cuisine and the evolution of flavors in Dutch gastronomy.

www.thedutchtable.com

Written and maintained by Dutch-American writer and cook Nicole Holten, The Dutch Table is a living record of traditional Dutch cuisine. Her site is a great reference for recipes and tips on Dutch baking, cooking, and gardening.

www.cbs.nl

The Statistics Netherlands (Centraal Bureau voor de Statistiek) website is a resource for statistical information about the Netherlands and its citizens. The organization was established in 1899 to collect and publish reliable data to aid in legislation and reduce inequality.

BOOKS

Halverhout, Heleen A. M. *Dutch Cooking.* **Drieholk Br Vitgevery De, 1972.**

To contrast the abundance and occasional eccentricity of Dutch cuisine prior to and during the Golden Age, Halverhout's simple book of Dutch recipes demonstrates the effects of economic decline and a long period of instability in Europe on the cuisine of the Netherlands. While the recipes themselves are simple and wholesome, they represent a reformation in the tastes of a nation after a long period of austerity. One can see in this volume that the twentieth century was a period during which the focus was frugality and nutrition, with a modest approach to seasonings. The recipes are simple and accessible to the home cook, but tend to be limited in their ingredients and variety.

Rose, Peter G. *The Sensible Cook: Dutch Foodways in the Old and the New World.* **Syracuse University Press, 1989.**

Peter Rose is a food historian, and her particular interest is in the first wave of Dutch immigrants to North America and their lives in New Netherland. Her translation of *De Verstandige*

Kock (The Sensible Cook), the cookery-focused volume of the larger *Het Vermakelijk Landtleven (The Pleasurable Country Life)*, is a unique look at the cuisine and culture of wealthy Dutch families in the seventeenth century. It is here that readers can glimpse what life was like for people of means during a period of economic prosperity in the Netherlands. The recipes are in some cases very modern, with emphasis on fresh, local vegetables, often steamed or cooked very quickly to preserve texture and taste; in some cases, they are indicative of the opulence of the times, with dishes that make use of several meats and spices at once. Although the book was printed in the Netherlands, it became very popular with migrants to North America.

Schama, Simon. *The Embarrassment of Riches: An Interpretation of Dutch Culture in the Golden Age.* **Vintage, 1987.**

A professor and historian at Columbia University in New York, Schama specializes in seventeenth-century Dutch art and European history. *The Embarrassment of Riches* is an epic, nearly 700-page overview of Dutch culture during the Golden Age, a period of wealth and progress in the Netherlands. It's a look at who the Dutch were at that time, from their view of themselves to their perspective on the world beyond their borders. It touches on Dutch anxieties around abundance and examines the country's art for insight into it's people's identity and values. The chapter "Feasting, Fasting and Timely Atonement" will be of interest to those curious about the moral value historically ascribed to certain foods and the lingering effects of moralism on modern Dutch cuisine.

van der Zeijst Bates, Johanna. *Let's Go Dutch.* **Van der Zeijst, 1989.**

For a generation of Dutch-Canadians and Dutch-Americans, *Let's Go Dutch* is the seminal volume on Dutch cuisine. The recipes have a very traditional feel to them, with a bit of North American flair. Bates's tone is warm and friendly, and she gives the impression of a kindly aunt walking you through the dishes she grew up with. The recipes demonstrate a nostalgia for home, but do their best to incorporate ingredients widely available at the time. For first- and second-generation North American children of Dutch parents, this book is an essential reference for the kind of old-world cuisine they might long for but not have access to. There aren't a lot of other Dutch cookbooks available in English. I recommend this book as a resource for understanding Dutch culture in North America, and the cuisine of the Dutch diaspora.

INDEX

PHOTO: BETHANY SCHIEDEL

EMILY WIGHT is a writer and recipe developer. Her work has appeared in *Room, SAD Mag, OCW, Vancouver Magazine,* in anthologies, and online. Her first cookbook, *Well Fed, Flat Broke: Recipes for Modest Budgets and Messy Kitchens,* was published by Arsenal Pulp Press in 2015. Her blog is at well-fedflatbroke.com; you can also connect with her on Facebook (facebook.com/WellFedFlatBroke) or on Instagram (insta-gram.com/emvandee). She lives in Vancouver.